Body Language

The words say what is right to say, the body what is true!!

How to Analyze People, Use Powerful Communication, Manipulation and Negotiation Skills to Influence Anyone. Understand Behavioral Psychology to Win in Business and Relationships.

Edward J.P. Aniston

TABLE OF CONTENTS

Introduction

Congratulations on purchasing your copy of *Body Language* and thank you for doing so.

There are plenty of books on this subject, so thanks again for choosing this one! We made sure that this is the best comprehensive body language guide available on the market, so please enjoy and discover the secret to reading others' thoughts through their gestures and much more!

What separates Homo sapiens from mere animal? Science tells us quite unanimously: "the ability to communicate." However, we must first distinguish the signals that set humans apart from animals. For example, a single warning call can cause a group of animals to flee.Both humans and animals experience this communication process. The situation is different when the command, "Please follow me to the salon!" causes a group of people to "follow" the speaker, in both meanings of the word. The animals' warning call is an analog signal; the above sentence, however, consists of several digital signals. WATZLAWICKS states that there are basically two types of signals: analog signals that are direct, pictorial, and analogous, and digital signals that are symbolic, abstract, often "complicated," and probably specific to humans.

A child is able to associate the words "Woof woof" and "dog" much faster with the animal, because the "Woof woof" is an analogy to a barking dog. Digital signals have to be laboriously learned before they can be understood and applied. The more your "Woof woof" sounds like barking, the more analogous your signals become. "Dog," on the other hand, is the digital information that is just as little common to the animal it's supposed to describe has, like the words "dog," "chien," or "cane."

Anyone who has not been able to speak the local language abroad knows how direct and problem-free analog communication often is. Let's say you want five packs of cigarettes. You have discovered a brand that you can interpret. So, your body language tells the dealer what you want. You can also display the number analogously by holding up five fingers. Whether the salesman converts this analog signal into "five" or something else, i.e. another digital signal, is irrelevant. Your portrayal of five is five-kind, so he understands you. For this, WATZLAWICKS (88) quotes a brilliant sentence from Bateson and Jackson: "The number five (has) nothing in particular five-fold in itself and the word "table" has nothing particularly table-like": the human being can communicate both digitally and analogously, although digital signals have to be learned before they can be understood or applied. You can express many things only digitally, and others only analogously. The very fact that man can use both types of communication makes him, in the opinion of science, homo sapiens!

We cannot send content-level signals without "sending in" analog signals from the relational level; no one can speak without a tone of voice, facial expressions, or gestures. Everyone hesitates. We always relay a certain attitude that can be interpreted, and so on.

Therefore, most of us have never learned to perceive signals on the relational level to the same extent. So, we usually miss many signals that could say "more" to us. We usually react unconsciously, intuitively, emotionally to the few analog signals we perceive, right? However, if you learn to consciously direct your attention to these signals, then you will receive two major advantages. First, you will be able to recognize when your relationship with another person is deteriorating, allowing you to "intercept" and tactically adjust to it. It is probably obvious that this ability can benefit both your professional and personal life!

Second, you will also be able to check your consciously registered observations. So, you will then be able to use a performance control as you learn that analog signals are not always clear. As WATZLAWICKS (88) points out, the signals "tears," "smiles," or a "clenched fist" are not clearly translated as "pain," "joy," or "combative aggression." Because you can shed tears of joy, you can also smile arrogantly or embarrassedly, and the clenched fist can also show self-discipline and an effort to avoid a fight! The same is true of silence. You can be silent because you think, because you reject a statement, because you hope the other person will speak, because you want to emphasize your next words, or out of insecurity. How easily one can misunderstand analog signals of the body! Well, no more,since you have this book or ebook reader in your hands!

You are now probably starting to wonder the extent to which the knowledge of "body language" from the field of Kinesis is scientifically founded or really proven.

This question conveys a certain need for security. One would like to think that what one knows or is about to learn is "really true." And one often thinks that the label "scientifically proven" can provide a kind of guarantee.

Of course, I try to provide body language information that I think is "safe," which, in my opinion, is most likely "correct." Nevertheless, certain conclusions that I draw may also be wrong. EINSTEIN once wrote in a letter to POPPER that scientific theories are ultimately never logically inferred but can only be invented, and that every scientist or author always creates laws to some extent from facts and observations interpreted and explained in a unique way! Apart from that, mental models do not necessarily have to be "right" to ensure practical and/or material benefits. Many have already sailed for "India" to arrive instead in "America"! For example, Newtonian physics not only revolutionized (and falsified) the previous view of the world, but it also stimulated unprecedented developments – before EINSTEIN's falsification and improvement of NEWTON's world view brought us a step further.

Perhaps our current approaches in Kinesics are ultimately Newtonian approaches. Maybe tomorrow or the next day an "Einstein" will come around, who will approach our knowledge differently and, therefore, come to differentiated or completely new approaches. It stands out on the Horizon of interdisciplinary research developments, the one hint at an almost Einstein-like approach! Nevertheless, we can work with our current knowledge in daily practice. NEWTON's physics lasted 200 years and gave many practical advantages before being falsified and improved. Kinesics is only several decades old, but experts have already proven how useful it is when applied to daily practice!

I hope that you will consider using such a benefit from the information in this book. That's exactly what we're aiming for, and you will not want to miss the chance to discover the secret to reading others' thoughts through their gestures and much more!

Part 1: The Perception – Body Language Signals

Photo by Anthony DeRosa

The first impression is the one that will never be

forgotten!!!

.........Which one do you want to show off ?

Chapter 1: Basics of Targeted Perception

1.1 The Impression

It is an interesting fact that human beings perceive rapid successive stimuli not as a series of stimuli but as an overall picture. You can test this by experimenting with a burning cigarette in the dark: when you "draw" a circle by moving the cigarette slowly, you will see the circular motion. Perform the same movement with lightning speed, then only perceive the shape (the circle itself). This observation is easiest if you look in a mirror while trying.

This phenomenon is explained by the fact that the brain is constantly trying to find what is recognizable, to bring order into (apparent) disorder, to complete incomplete things, etc. However, this happens so fast that we are not aware of these processes. That's why you perceived the overall figure "circle" in the experiment.

It also happens to us when we get to know or meet a person. Although an abundance of information units can be arranged at lightning speed, we consciously only experience the overall picture. We speak of the person making an impression, not a bene: a single impression, although this "one" impression actually consists of countless strung-together partial impressions.

So, we register at the sight of a person z. As physique, posture, facial expressions, gestures successively, but perceive this process as "simultaneously" because it runs so fast. Should the person speak at the moment, we would also include the tone of voice, the speech melody, the rhythm of the speech, the volume, any dialectal colorations, and much more in our overall picture, to take our "one" impression with us. A good observer can register a lot more at the "first" look, e.g. a stain on the clothing, a particularly clear pronunciation that the person would need a shave or nervously playing with the lighter and much more.

Since this overall impression is not composed of a single but of many different partial bits of information, the question arises as to which (partial) impression was "really" the first. Some authors assume that the very first impression must emanate from the physique, while others put in this place the attitude of a person. Still, others believe that the facial expressions (especially the eyes) had the fastest effect on an observer. However, we are idle about this question, precisely because the sequence is so fast that we cannot clearly describe it. That is, the order of these partial impressions is (at least not) exactly ascertainable. So, whether you register a person's physique a nanosecond before the posture or vice versa, I think it's an academic question.

1.2 Physique and Posture

However, another question might be important for daily practice, namely: Does the impact of a person's physique contribute more to the overall impression than posture, or vice versa? Again, the discussion in professional circles is still in progress. Personally, I tend to think that information that has more practical value changes more quickly (or that we are most likely to influence ourselves). Since this obviously applies to the posture, we will prefer this train of thought to the physique hypothesis. It should also be remembered that the "knowledge" about the physique can trigger a kind of Pygmalion effect (see Introduction) on itself. So, I knew z. For example, in America, a man whom we call Billy S. He was a follower of KRETSCHMER's theory of the relationship between physique and character (51).

According to this theory, Billy S. now thought that he had to be cheerful and sociable since he was a pronounced endomorph. In reality, however, he suffered from this description, which he regarded as a demand. He accepted her because, in his opinion, she was "scientific" (that is, decisive for him). That is, Billy did not suffer because he was an endomorph but because the definition contradicted his nature. However, believing that a scientist knew more about his "type" than he could ever know, he lived in constant conflict because he found it difficult to live the "required" behavior.

It must be pointed out that, of course, KRETSCHMER's definitions do not contain any demands. The problem arose only because Billy S. took this description as a demand. But this also proved to be true to that part of KRETSCHMER's typology, which states that endomorphs tend to be sad and have mood swings. To what extent this second statement represents an aspect of every endomorph or to what extent Billy S. pointed him out because he believed the first statement, is difficult to determine.

In any case, Billy S. is a good example of the dilemma of a person who "confuses himself with his definition," as WATTS puts it (87). Whether this "definition" comes about through demands of education (be it so-and-so) or through expectations that we ourselves set ourselves, the result is the same: an inner disruption, lack of harmony, vague or strong feelings of displeasure, of failure, of dissatisfaction, in short: conflicts.

1.3 Self-Knowledge

Incidentally, when Billy S. took the course in which he was confronted with the type theorem of KRETSCHMER, he was not looking for more self-knowledge but sought more knowledge of others. This shows that one cannot turn to topics of applied human knowledge without at the same time learning more about oneself and one's own signals. That is why I think it is particularly important to emphasize once again that our information does not constitute "absolute truths" or that even information that you believe to be right does not constitute a requirement. A human does not have to be happy just because he is fat and because we believe he has discovered a law that correlates to being fat with happiness!

Nevertheless, we assume that our information is (for the time being) "correct." But, as Hume's famous induction problem so wonderfully demonstrates, we can never assume that anything can ever really be "proven" with certainty. What applies to the sunrise, of course, also applies to body language signals (see Introduction).

1.4 Laws of Body Language

Let us assume that you have learned through experience or theoretical discourse: "Clenched lips mean that the person (at the moment) does not let in anything from the environment and does not want to let anything into the environment. "

Thousands of observations in the past, in which a squeezed mouth might really mean self-closing-to-the-environment, prove nothing about the person whose mouth you are going to notice tomorrow or the day after tomorrow!

The importance of this train of thought cannot be emphasized clearly enough (see Introduction). For the inadmissible conclusion after HUME of this kind led z. For example, ARISTOTLE assumed that the brightest people had the smallest heads, whereas GALL claimed the opposite about 200 years ago. Zeddies (94) says:

"From GALL's time comes ... the erroneous opinion that is still heard today ... that the 'spirit', i.e. here as much as intelligence, is expressed in the high forehead. The genius must distinguish itself from the unspiritual man by a particularly high forehead; the "high forehead" after that is almost an infallible sign of "high spirit" ... The physician H. KRUKENBERG once pointed out how the doctrine of GALL and the conception of his Time has influenced the meaning of the 'spirit' even in the form of the ... (skull) form. While GOETHE, as can still be clearly seen on silhouettes and especially on the picture published in 1777/78, had a backward, fleeting forehead, especially benevolent portraitists endowed GOETHE with such a powerful forehead in his last years that his head was almost the type of a water-head could apply."

Now, perhaps the question arises of how useful theories on applied knowledge of human nature (in this case: on body language) in view of the previous discussion because now, they "really" are. Answer: It is true that the likelihood that a squeezed mouth will contain the same information about self-closing tomorrow is very high, but you can never be completely "sure." Therefore, extreme caution is required when it comes to making certain regularities of body language expressions "laws." As MAGEE states in his wonderful introduction to

POPPER's Thought (58), the word "law" is ambiguous (in almost all the languages I've studied so far!). While a law in the legal sense certainly includes a claim, this is clearly not the case with laws, as scientists put it. This fact, MAGEE says, is often overlooked and then leads to misconceptions, expectations, or fallacies. Because a (natural) law (or a "rule") cannot be "hurt" because it is not a demand but a description attempt. Unlike a law in the legal meaning, which includes both a concrete claim and can be transgressed!

1.5 Error Always Possible!

For our daily practice, this means: If one thinks that he has recognized or accepted the "law" or the "rule" behind his mouth, then one must not assume that every mouth that is compressed must always comply with our law! That's why it's so important to work with control questions. This is the only way to check on a case-by-case basis whether your own impression is "right" here as well.

Now, follow a "law" which I hope you will understand and accept as a requirement:

If the practiced thinks that he has "understood" body language signals, he tries to control (instead of assuming) those that he has seen through the other one!

Just as the experienced hikers can learn to distinguish signals of the arrogance from those of shyness (if it is even a form of arrogance that was not born out of insecurity). Only the success control makes it possible to determine whether one has correctly perceived. For even a single signal that has been overlooked can make the overall situation "completely different." It is this control that helps to verify that signals that you have perceived also have the meaning that you attribute to them. For example, turning a lateral head for people of other cultures means "yes," while in our latitudes this signal translates to "no" (the more you deal with people from foreign countries, the more important it becomes to you, signals whose content is different, we will come back to it later in the book).

Furthermore, the success control can avoid that one wrongly refers to a signal, to his words, to the here and now. Often our words or actions (or something that the other is about to solve) resolve associations that have nothing at all to do with ourselves. Just as the word "price" (in our introduction) reminded the technician that he had forgotten to keep a promise!

Finally, signals can also contain no message. Thus, the nervous twitching of an eyelid can be held by the viewer for a wink. Depending on the overall situation, this may mean that the untrained person is pleased or angry about this apparent message.

1.6 A "Kinesics Dictionary"?

Now there are authors whose work on non-language signals is almost a "dictionary." There is then z. For example, what does it mean when someone puts his hand in his pocket? Furthermore, there is even to be read, which nuanced differences it makes, whether the hand is placed flat or concentrated in the pocket or what feeling you signal, if you keep your thumb inside or outside the pocket edge. Such considerations are wrong and a better understanding of body language is not helpful. For example, the fashion of flat pockets on such tight pants are not taken into account, which does not allow a clenched fist in the bag, or in which the thumb has no more space! The latter refers to the fact that someone who thinks he owns a "wordlist" will be far more inclined to believe that he has "seen through" the other. Many people are unconsciously aware of this belief when, like our advisor (see introduction), they immediately assume that they already have the right feeling for the non-verbal signals! So, you will be even less inclined to ask control questions! The latter only has one way to verify his observations. SCHOPENHAUER certainly meant that when he said: "The knowledge of the human being is an area in which one never learns and even the most experienced man often finds himself in error (94)."

But how was he to catch himself if he did not ask any questions? Without them, he would notice only a small portion of his mistakes, not enough to systematically learn from them.

1.7 Success Checks Enable Systematic Learning

Any system of applied human knowledge, from astrology to numerology, to "scientific" systems, is based on the trial and error method. One observes, evaluates the perceptions, and interprets them on the basis of any criteria that belong to the system. Then one examines his impression and either states that the interpretation was correct, or that it was wrong.

In the latter case one wonders why one was wrong, and next time one tries to avoid this error. This is exactly what POPPER's thesis of how human knowledge grows (see Introduction). Without a constant success control of this kind but no knowledge can grow!

1.8 Three Methods of Success Control

How do you bring this success control now? There are three options, the first being the easiest for most people. Of course, when you decide which kind of control to use, you have to decide for yourself, as this depends both on the personal style of the controlling person and on the conversation situation.

1.8.1 The Open Question

These are questions that cannot be answered with yes or no. This type of question has the strategic advantage of encouraging (almost forced to say) freedom of expression. However, the more words he speaks (e.g. by responding with one sentence), the greater our chance of reaching our goal. Namely both the content and the manner in which he speaks and hears (angry, doubtful, thoughtful). Assuming that after consulting the technician's "refusal" signals (see Introduction), our adviser had asked such a control question, the technician would have been able to explain to the consultant what he had just remembered. Thus, it would have been clear that the three "negative" signals had related neither to price nor to the here and now.

Open questions of this kind ask for an opinion. Formulations like the following are, among others, possibilities of such questions:

"How do you see that?"

"What do you mean?"

"What is your opinion on that?"

"What does that look like from your point of view?

Note: No control question is an often-heard formulation of a suggestive kind: "Surely you think that's fair?" (Or: "You agree with me?").

Although such leading questions have their strategic meaning, they should not be used as a control question in terms of body language signals as they neither really want nor make free expression of opinion. (Here, there is a danger of consent as a path of least resistance or contradiction when the other has seen through tactics.)

1.8.2 The Closed Question

Here one asks clearly and clearly whether one interpreted a signal correctly. A question that is of course not always suitable. In our case study, it would not have been cheap. But often that's the shortest way. For example:

"You seem upset?" Or, "I have the impression that something's wrong with you. Is that correct? "Or:" Does that seem to really please you? "

This question can also be used in business life, but only if the climate of conversation is particularly open and the two partners value each other. Otherwise, such a question can certainly be considered a breakthrough into the psychological private sphere. Psychologists, in particular, like to take on the wrath of their environment when they believe they have to translate all sorts of observations into such questions...

1.8.3 The Silence

Silence is even the method that achieves the best results but is difficult for most people to learn. If our counselor had simply kept silent when he had observed the three "negative" signals, then the technician would also have had a chance to speak up or quickly give his order before continuing the conversation. Because most people start to talk, if their counterpart is silent, I hold this method as the most successful, especially in professional life, when the second method is not applicable.

The method of silence also includes a technique that GORDON (36) calls active silence: one leaves a sentence unfinished in space. GORDON believes that people complete each other's sentences with words that have been repeated, but in terms of our control questions, these can also be our own words. For example, "Regarding the price, you may have already taken from the documents ...?"

If the other has taken it and has already resistance built up, he may perhaps speak angrily into the silence. But he can also be interested to ask or easily dismiss the price question. In our case study, the technician would also have had the opportunity to respond because of its association.

Probably the fact that this method is so effective (when it comes to learning more about the other) is an explanation that many psychoanalysts use almost constantly. SHEPARD, an American psychiatrist called this tactic in his book (79) – the HHM game. A variant of this is the fountain pen scratching or hissing game: Here, the analyst occasionally makes a sound to indicate that he has not fallen asleep, while the patient speaks constantly and his silence remains tact!

Try it yourself: As many control questions as possible over the next few days, determine if you can use the silence method. If it is (too) difficult for you, learn the other two techniques, i.e. the open or closed question. The latter can probably be used more frequently in the home than the former.

If later in this book we make certain statements about the meaning of a signal, then these are not to be regarded as a "list of words" for immediate translation, but always as an observation aid. Only your own performance control can determine from case to case whether the interpretation is correct.

But what do we want to pay attention to? What can we see, hear, perceive? If we accept that a "list of words" cannot be our goal, then the question arises of the "grammar" of body language. Which topics can we assign individual signals? How do we develop a feeling for the "sentence structure," i.e. for several signals that only express meaning when combined with each other? That's what it should be about in the following.

A word can try to explain who we are, a gesture
what

we want.

But only time will confirm both.

(cannovaV, Twitter)

Chapter 2: Criteria of Targeted Perception

2.1 Methods

In principle, there are two possibilities: The first method works with a variety of generic terms, e.g. For example, the signals "on the other side," "on the other hand," "on oneself," "psychosomatic signals" (such as blanching), etc. Such an approach allows the researcher, even the smallest signal elements (so-called Kinons) unmistakably to record and assign. It is used when kinetics spend months analyzing 8-minute strips of film.

The second method uses fewer generic terms, accepting that some signals cannot be classified as "clean" (We still come back to these "borderline cases."). Nevertheless, this method of working is suitable for observing processes that take place live

(live, alive), i.e. for living persons whose behavior can neither be considered slowed down nor repeated. Since we almost exclusively observe our daily lives, we will become part of the second method in this work serve. However, we are aware that our assignment is crude, although it allows for rapid analysis. And that's the point. What sense would an exact observation, which can only be formulated 40 seconds later, have in everyday practice? Nevertheless, we must resign ourselves to the fact that such a rough analysis must ultimately up to some extent remain imprecise. Our classification covers only five categories.

2.2 Five Criteria

2.2.1 Attitude

By this, we mean both the posture that a person is currently taking and movements that alter or influence posture, such as a shifting of the body weight in itself forward or backward bending, a seesaw on the ball of the foot, a rolling over of the legs, etc.

2.2.2 Facial Expressions

By this, we mean all phenomena that we can observe in the face of a person, including psychosomatic processes such as: For example, blushing.

2.2.3 Gesture

By this, we mean all the gestures of the poor, the "language of the hands," as well as many acts such as: Opening a door, expressing a cigarette, etc.

2.2.4 Distance

By this, we mean the distance that one takes to others (sometimes also to animals or objects), as well as sudden movements, which have a change of the distance to the goal, e.g. a sudden one-step-retreat, etc. (Here we already see possibilities for borderline signals: Should we see the retreat as a change of attitude or interpret it in relation to distance?) We will come back to that again.

2.2.5 Tone of Voice

By this we mean all manifestations manifesting in speech insofar as our analysis does not focus on the content of what has been said. The tone, the speech melody, pauses, volume, speech rhythm, etc. The tone we also include vocalizations without verbal content, such. For example, clicking on the tongue, sighing, moaning, etc.

2.3 Assignment of Signals (Pre-Exercise)

In practice, the assignment must happen at lightning speed, as the situation we want to observe constantly changes. That's what we mean by the term "live" observation. The term has quickly come to be used to distinguish living ("real") situations from recorded (rerun) or long-stored (canned) situations. And this element of the living forces us quickly and accurately to work. Therefore, it is advisable to practice in the "dry course," i.e. now! In the seminar, it usually takes about 10 minutes, until the participants arbitrarily categorized signals either immediately or can quickly determine as a "borderline case." The following is, therefore, a pre-exercise: Please try to assign the list of non-linguistic signals below to the five categories posture, facial expressions, gestures, spacing, and pitch. All signals are "hidden" in a sentence that slightly outlines or hints at the overall situation. Example: "She smiled dreamily." Analysis: Mimic

He shouted: "One day I want to experience it, that you do what you have been told! "
She took a step back, "So do you imagine that before?!"
He stood casually leaning against the buffet, his right foot over the ankle of his left. After four-year-old Belinda had assured her mother that she could button her coat alone, her mother said, "Of course

you can, my darling! " While at the same time sheath, the little ones buttoned themselves.

While NIXON claimed to be in contact with the young people, he stretched out both arms several times defensively, as if to push them away from him.

She waited, bobbing on the balls of her feet until the helper filled out the form.

He went to the window and opened it.

She looked at him silently, her nostrils with restrained excitement quivering.

The coffee was so hot that he spit it reflexively.

He said ironically: "Always let the clutch pedal whiz very fast, which is extremely good for the transmission." (After Watzlawick, 88).

Well, did you find the preliminary exercise easy?

2.4 Verbalization of Perception

The following tasks include the most essential exercises for a better understanding of the body language signals at all! The translation of intuitive, mostly unconscious interpretations into analytical, conscious thinking requires a verbalization of non-verbal processes. This in-word clipping of observations that were previously registered below the word threshold is very easy for some signals, but for others, it seems almost impossible at first. This is why anthropologists and kinesics have invented their own symbolic language by which they capture these non-verbal signals. Although we do not want to work that exactly, a translation into our word language is necessary, because, without such a description, no conscious analysis is possible. Also reading a text about body language is as meaningless as reading a score for one who is not very familiar with the symbols used!

Therefore, if possible, perform the following tasks until you can do each one quickly and easily. After all, here too, the old rule applies: either it is easy for the practitioner, then it goes so fast that there is no reason to not do the exercise. Or it falls something difficult (he), then the need to practice just this aspect the hand, provided one wants his knowledge of the body language to be put to practical use in the practice also!

2.5 The Empathy

How often do we say, "If I were you," and I mean in reality, "If I, I were in one place like yours ...." It's not easy to feel what it's like in someone else's shoes. What do you think of the following rule?

Someone who cannot become aware of their own body language signals will never be able to register the signals of others very accurately. Body language analysis requires not only a "sharp" (read: trained) gaze and a "good" (i.e. trained) ear, but probably a much higher degree of good "sense."
This word describes a good empathy without which any method of self and human knowledge will fail. (You may also know someone who has attended 30 seminars and has read 500 books on the subject and

yet does not get beyond a certain limit?) Registering one's own feelings and non-verbal signals means going through two essential processes:

First, one perceives a signal, e.g. For example, one tugs nervously on the lip. Second, you register how you feel right now. This combination helps one later tote others guess what feeling may have triggered a certain signal with them. Of course, this guessing is commonly called 'interpret' because it sounds 'scientific'. However, the fact remains that scientists must also "guess" as long as they work on a theory of knowledge, that is, create. Empathy for others can, therefore, be practiced by registering one's own processes. We can express this again as a rule:

The more empathy a person has with their own emotional world, the more they will be able to develop for others.

And vice versa. This rule also explains why especially sensitive people not only have much understanding for others but are also very sensitive (sometimes mimosa-like) to others. This brings us to the next task for you.

2.6 Exercise

Try to capture your own body language signals with a running commentary (like a "raging reporter"). You can do this both mentally through speech-thinking, as well as loud, maybe even on tape? You could also use such a recording for the additional exercise under 2.10 if you also want to do this exercise. (It is not part of the "official" exercise cycle and will only be suitable for some of the readers.) Finally, you can do this exercise in writing, if you want to use it in the sense of a self-inventory, to highlight your eventual peculiarities to come.

For about 10-15 minutes, try to describe every aspect of body language you can discover. For example: "I'm wrinkling my forehead, my lips are pressed against each other, I run purposefully towards the kitchen, my back feels cramped, I notice that I'm standing on one leg, I'm operating the coffee machine ..." Try to detect signals of each category!

2.7 Active Body Language

Sometimes it can be of great benefit to be able to actively use or actively limit one's body language. Maybe you would like to learn to avoid a nervous signal or to use a signal whose utility is obvious to you, even though you have seldom used this signal in the past, e.g. Eye contact. If you are interested, the following additional exercise is recommended:

Speak a series of body language signals as an instruction on a tape (or take the tape of the above problem). In case of doubt, text templates can be found in "Groschenromanen" if you cannot think of enough things, as this genre uses a wealth of body language signals so as not to strain the reader's imagination! Of course, instead of a tape recording, a second person can also preach or read the instructions.

Now they try to comply with all requests immediately and without hesitation. A situation that every actor, every model has to master. As a variant, the imitation of other people is also suitable, be it present or seen on television. If you declare this as a party game, on the one hand, you can have a lot of fun, on the other hand, you can train your skills! By the way, in a group, you will find that this exercise is very easy for some people, while others can barely grasp the grossest movements. Which type do you belong to?

2.8 Exercise

What we have not yet trained is our hearing. In order to develop a feeling for the tone of voice, we have to listen differently than before. The easiest way to do this is to start with a TV program, a suitable one.

Newscasts, of course, contain fewer sound nuances than a movie, but that's best stated for yourself. Watch TV and try to verbalize tone signals. For example, "He speaks loudly, aggressively, hesitantly, slowly," etc. Here you will find again that more nuanced perceptions only appear with the exercise that they then perform as well as a barely noticeable hesitation, a slight vibration of the voice and the like can perceive and verbalize!

2.9 Transmission Effect in Daily Practice

Completing these exercises will not only help you because you are training individual aspects, but the main purpose is to have a transient effect on your daily practice. Suddenly you start to see "through different eyes." They also consciously perceive nuances in the tone of voice or the pausing of a speaker. So that the Bible wisdom: "Seek and you will find" will come true again. You will perceive more in the future because you are searching consciously!

Signals that you are now consciously registering, instead of as previously unconscious.

2.10 Completion

Exercise: At the end of our exercise cycle, which dealt with perception, categorization, and verbalization, another task in which all previous steps are summarized. Put yourself in a situation where you can observe both yourself and other people. (Your living room with a running TV would also be such a situation, for example.)

Now you consciously perceive, verbalize, and categorize. This time you pay attention to the signals of others (or the characters on TV) as well as to your own as well as in daily practice too. Of course, you cannot verbalize almost all the signals that occur simultaneously. That's why this exercise has another, very practical aspect: you have to select. (We always do.) By perceiving and interpreting the one signal, other signals escape you. That is normal. Further, you will perceive an interesting jump from own signals to those of others and back. Again, this is a normal aspect of body language assessment in practice

2.11 Case: A Protocol Study

Mr. M. mumbles "This is crap." (Tone.) My right neighbor looks at him disapprovingly (facial expressions). I smile while (facial expressions). Mrs. Birkenbihl walks slowly (attitude or action?). Mr. Y. looks over his shoulder at her (facial expressions) and covers his log (gesture) so she cannot read anything (speculation). She did not even try! I'm already smiling again (facial expressions). I seem to grin a lot here in the seminar (Ahem). Now Mr. M. stares to himself (facial expressions). He cannot think of anything (or should I say)? That's speculation, of course. Now I should be able to ask a control question. Ha! Suddenly I notice my left knee bobbing back and forth (posture or gesture?) - I think I've been doing that for a while. The aunt next door chews on her pen (facial expressions or gestures?). She always does that when we have to write something. If she knows that? The neighbor of her looks at her (facial expressions). She does not seem to notice (?). Mrs. Birkenbihl tugs at her upper lip (gesture). Now she looks at the clock (gesture, because of an action?). Me too (gesture with me!). Two minutes left. Mr. M. has just thrown the pen, ostentatious (gesture)! Now he leans back demonstratively (his attitude, my interpretation!). My neighbor looks at him again disapprovingly (facial expressions). His behavior is often disapproving. Is he aware of that? I'm just realizing that my knee is twitching again (apparently a gesture?). Mr. M. just yawned loudly (tone?). He sends many signals to show that he wants to stand out from us (distance from him, speculation on my part). I'll talk to him in the coffee break on it (plot, planned, ha!). My left hand holds the paper convulsively (gesture). Aha, my knee dangles again (certainly gestures!). I'll have to keep that in mind ... time is up.

We have seen that again borderline cases occur here. However, it does not matter which category we assign a signal to, as long as we have first perceived it and secondly verbalized it. The knowledge of these generic terms should only represent a frame of reference in our mind, both make it easier to perceive and allows us to communicate through body language.

Do you know how to remove the mask......

......or how to put it on?

Do you know how to read your interlocutor's mind

and if he's wearing a mask?

Chapter 3: Criteria of Assessment

3.1 Anders Perceive

Surely you have already experienced the phenomenon that a word that you've learned just now to understand, suddenly permanently "turns up." It's as if newspapers, radio, television, books, and fellow human beings have conspired to use this vocabulary all the time. In fact, in all likelihood, the word had previously been used just as often, but we have overheard or missed it.

Something similar will happen to you now with regard to the body language signals. You will be amazed at the abundance of information that comes to you from all sides! Maybe you have already noticed this effect. But you do not just want to perceive more, but also use these perceptions practically.

However, if you want to evaluate, analyze, interpret, or even refine (please do not judge), you need criteria. Without standards one cannot measure, without a prescription of what one wants to examine, no results can arise. Our generic terms posture, facial expressions, gestures, distance, and tone were perceptual criteria that serve us (similar to auxiliary lines) to make us an "image." If we can now perceive and verbalize a signal, then we have taken the necessary first step with it: we have described (see preface). However, our verbalization does not say anything about the signal's rating.

But what do we want to know? Which priorities do we want to set? What can we pay attention to?

Any "statement" that someone will give you now will change the way you and others see you in the future, and so on. You can strongly influence this. Therefore,

I would like to ask you to regard the following train of thought as just one possible approach. There are others. Determine your own reactions when reading. Be especially critical. Because in this chapter, in fact, it's about a philosophical question: "What should one pay attention to when judging oneself and others?" One person considers spontaneity to be an important criterion, another honesty, and the other places great value on self-discipline (so that he will rate spontaneity differently from the one that seemed so valuable to them). Further, someone may find it important that the observed signals correspond to his notions of "good behavior" because he considers politeness an important criterion. Such a person is more likely to judge the other's yawning as "negative," especially when executed without a hand or even to interpret this signal as rudeness towards him, that is, as a "hostile" signal.

Ultimately everyone has to decide for themselves which priorities to set, but often a discussion about possible criteria helps to define their own more precisely!

3.2 Honesty / Sincerity

This is a criterion that is consistently considered by most seminar participants to be the "main criterion." I would like to advise caution here. First, how honest is "honest"? Second, do you have a clear answer to the question of whether "absolute" honesty could sometimes be very hurtful, and to what extent it should be sought after? Third, are you so sure you never lie to yourself or others?!?! (Be it insecurity or embarrassment, be it in the form of a "polite" lie, or because you may not want to believe something?) Interestingly enough, I have often found that those who put so much emphasis on catching others in the event of lies, not always understanding it with the truth. Here is the psychoanalytic conclusion that they, because they deduce themselves from others, are so afraid of the dishonesty of others. Also, if someone lies out of fear of the consequences, or because he does not want to hurt another, then the motives are completely different. The "truth fanatics" usually ignore this, precisely because they have not given enough thought to the criterion of honesty!

3.3 Congruence / Incongruence

Of course, every signal always refers to the situation in which the looking person is currently located. Incongruence can therefore mean:

1. A discrepancy to the spoken words (see NIXON example, introduction).

2. A discrepancy between an observed signal and our expectation: Assuming you give someone a present and expect a pleasing response, but see that the other is disappointed or depressed. This would be such an incongruence.

3. A discrepancy between an observed signal and our expectation can also lead to pseudo-

incongruence if the other one has no idea what we might have expected. In the example above, the recipient knows that the giver hopes he will be happy. It is different when you expect a reaction that the others cannot guess. Either because you think he has some information that he (still) does not have. Or because it comes from a different culture and will, therefore, send "unexpected" signals that may seem incongruent to us, even though they are not (in his view).

4. A discrepancy to the person. Franz Josef Strauss was expected in certain situations, so to speak, certain signal groups. The better you know a person, the more likely you are to be able to predict your analog signals. However, if these are completely different now, then we say that the person is not "herself" today. This is what we mean by incongruence with the person.

5. Lately, there is an incongruence factor in gestures that, strictly speaking, are not. Some people wave completely unmotivated in the air or hit the table in a steady rhythm, although they do not say anything that should be "underpinned." These analog signals seem to have no relation to the words and are therefore also perceived as incongruent.

3.4 Spontaneity / Self-Discipline

The more spontaneous a reaction, the less thoughtful it is. If honesty and sincerity are important, spontaneity will be more "positive" than self-discipline. Now the signals are always "embedded" in the overall situation, so that there may well be moments when free, open, informal, spontaneous behavior may seem "more positive" than restrained, disciplined behavior. Furthermore, those who always consider spontaneity to be "better" in case of doubt should be aware that tactlessness was also very spontaneous. Tactlessness is just a reaction that someone sent out before thinking about his words! That's why I sometimes silently amuse myself about a person I know who on the one hand demands that one should always be spontaneous, but at the same time very lightly offended if her brother violates her spontaneously with one of his "indiscretions." From this, we can once again see how difficult it is to create "absolute" standards for assessing body language signals (or standards for assessing each behavior!).

3.5 Positive / Negative

Of course, we perceive individual signals as "good" or "bad," i.e. we classify them immediately and usually unconsciously as "positive" or "negative." It must be clear that this is an extremely subjective description of the world and our fellow human beings. Whether a behavior is spontaneous or controlled, can be measured with a different scale than "good" or "bad" signals. So, if someone classifies a yawn of the other as disinterest and thus as negative, then he has judged very subjective. First, he assumes that the other yawns only when he has no interest (maybe he closes it to others?)! Secondly, he may feel the signal "negative" because it is "rude." Especially with the label "rude," one must be aware that all the rules of behavior are fixed on certain cultures and certain epochs of time. In Erasmus von ROTTERDAM1 (26), for example: "When two fingers fall down on the ground with two fingers, it must immediately be kicked out with the foot," both our two-fingered sniveling was considered rude (negative) also the leakage of nasal mucus. A second example with ROTTERDAM, however, has survived the times so far and could still be in a book of manners today: "Some.... have to scratch their heads or drill around in their teeth or gesticulate wildly with their hands and play with the knife (at a table). Or they have to cough and snort and spit. All this basically comes from a peasant embarrassment and looks like some kind of weirdness." One final example is intended to clarify two things: First, how little conscious is one's behavior or signals that seem "wrong" to be immediately negatively classified, i.e. emotionally angry or injured responding to them. This reaction is best shown by those norms that you normally do not talk about anymore. They are so natural (programmed) that we are already upset when someone brings them up. Secondly, the more often someone has to deal with people from other (sub-) cultures, the greater the danger that he will be quick as lightning unconsciously finds certain signals "bad" and lets them perceive them negatively-as long as he is not aware of this danger and can stand up to it. The last example:

"Some prescribe that the boy 'retains a tight buttocks blasts,' but one can thereby contract an illness."

How seldom do we consciously think that one has to hold back himself these days? This is clearly a norm that is hardly ever verbalized. Nevertheless, we react immediately if someone does not obey them, or if someone, after "it" happened to him, does not immediately send the "corresponding" analog signals, that is to say: dismayed at how embarrassing he is! But once you have the opportunity to sit with Bedouin, you would be angry with these people if you looked upset because these people do not accept your standard ... so it would be best to have this permanent classification in "good" or "positive" (or "negative") and therefore, we could get it under control. For one thing, because we always feel annoyed or hurt when we have a negative signal. This means that we are now producing combat hormones and wasting unnecessary energies into the process of having a "rage in the stomach." To a lesser extent, this also applies to any slight annoyance of course. On the other hand, because some signals in the eyes of the other cannot be "negative" at all if they start from different norms and customs than we do. However, these feelings of displeasure on our part are accompanied by negative signals, which we now send on a relationship level, which of course worsens the relationship and "poisons" the atmosphere of conversation. The "poison" are our fighting hormones (see "Joy through Stress" (7a) and Psycho-Logically Right Negotiation (7b).

3.6 Joke and Irony

As we have seen, the father meant the opposite when he advised the son to keep the eagle-owl lying around openly (introduction). Likewise, the words of the driving instructor (according to Watzlawick) should not be taken "seriously" when he says: "Always let the clutch pedal soar abruptly, which is enormously good for the transmission."

Now there are people who take everything very seriously. That's why the idea does not come to them, someone might want to make a joke. If the "ironic tone" is hinted at only slightly, it may well be that such persons "fall for" the digital signals. That's why the environment loves to "hug" them. For someone like that, the question of how serious someone might have meant something is a useful criterion. In particular, when one has more to do with people whose "dry humor" is accompanied by such weak analog signals that only a trained person will hear the irony or sarcasm. But sarcasm can be so hurtful when it uttered evil things in a tone that sounds so "sober," so "rational," so "objective."

You could list more criteria. But, first of all, there are many more in subgroups already mentioned and, secondly, unfortunately, we cannot go into the ethical systems that must be subject to any criteria choice. Our little discussion should only help you to determine the criteria by which you can judge. Of course, this decision is up to you! Another criterion will be discussed before we turn to the signals themselves:

3.7 Only A Single Signal?

There are situations in which success control is impossible. For example, if we judge the analog signals of a politician on television, or if we do not want to interrupt someone. An essential criterion is the question that on how many (or which) signals you support your assessment? Although there are sometimes individual signals that already have meaningfulness (we still come back to them), in general, they represent an exceptional case. Because the basic rule is rather:

A signal alone has no significance!

In particular, this applies to "small" signals such as the lifting of an eyebrow, which can have a variety of causes. Therefore, I consider statements by some authors to be dangerous, who already want to interpret the hand-in-the-bag plug-in alone, or who claim that just the way someone holds his cigarette already has clear explanatory power. Maybe such a signal can give us a hint, but just a hint, not the sole one! For example, brandishing a cigarette with a burning cigarette in front of your eyes may be an indication that he may not respect someone else's genital area. If we now include this hint in our targeted observation, it may be that we notice other signals pointing in the same direction. Or else he often intervenes in the "space of another" (both literally and figuratively), or else he takes objects of others without asking, i.e. only such a signal group can contain a certain significance.

Exceptions to this rule are pronounced, strongly striking gestures that are clearly in contradiction to what has been said, as in the NIXON example (where we also used additional information for interpretation!). Furthermore, all abrupt changes in body posture are considered an exception to the rule. As a conclusion to the interpretation, before we tackle these, one more word of the great geneticist BIRDWHISTELL.

No physical posture or movement has an exact meaning per se. Body language and languages are interdependent.

Ultimately, this means nothing else than that we must simultaneously perceive and describe the signals of the content and relationship levels if we want to "interpret" a gesture or another non-speech signal.

Part 2: The Interpretation – Body Language Signals

Image by mohamed Hassan

Those who must communicate always face the same problem: what to say and how to say it.
(Bill Gates)

No mouth is large enough to pronounce the whole thing.

(Alan Watts)

Chapter 4: Attitude

4.1 Experiments on Posture

In order to intensify the feeling for the essential statements of this chapter, I invite you to a series of mini-experiments (duration approx. 15 minutes). In the best case, read the following text only after completing these exercises.

In terms of execution, you have two options: Either you pimp the book so that you can read and execute one instruction at a time before continuing to read and work. Individual trains of thought are visually separated from each other by the word "stop" and one empty line each. Or you can have each statement read by another person, pausing on each blank line until you have given a signal indicating that you are ready for the next step.

If you want to learn a lot from this mini-cycle, then, of course, you could record your experiences after each experiment. This would be both a deepening of your ability to verbalize (see Chapter 2) and a good record of your own signals, which you can then use in the following versions to interpret them as well! Are you in a room where you can both stand free and take a few steps back and forth? Do you have a chair without armrests? Then we can start.

4.1.1 How Do You Stand?

Stand in the way you normally stand (e.g. when you are thinking about something or waiting for someone).

Stop.

Stay in that posture and become aware of how you stand: Are you resting your weight (usually) on both legs, on one leg? Do you shift your weight regularly from one leg to the other?

Stop.

Feel your focus! Where is he? In the head, chest, abdomen, back, buttocks or legs or feet?

Stop.

(If you want to take notes, write down the answers to the questions above.)

4.1.2 Do You Feel Your Muscles Standing Up?

Again, stand up straight (not stiff, but as "straight" as you usually do). Then slowly and consciously shift the weight of your upper body forward until you almost fall over.

Stop.

Repeat this movement and remain in this posture for a moment. Feel aware of which muscle parts you need to stretch where and how much to avoid falling over.

Stop.

(If you want to take notes, make a note of your observations now.)

4.1.3 Same Again, But Different, Please!

Again, you will shift your body weight, but now back to register which muscle parts need to be strained where and how strong so you do not fall over.

Stop.

(If you want to take notes, now ...)

4.1.4 How Are You Sitting?

Please sit on a chair without armrests, which is free in the room, so that you can lean on nowhere.

Stop.

How are you sitting? Where does your body focus on sitting? In front of, above or behind the pelvis (if you would pull up a straight line from the pelvis)?

Stop.

(If you want to take notes, now ...)

4.1.5 Posture A

Now sit on the outermost front edge of the chair and shift your body weight forward.

Stop.

You will find that your feet are most likely parallel now. Modify this by placing them in a step position, one foot more forward than the other.

Stop.

Now lower your head slightly and let your hands hang loosely between your knees. How do you feel now?

Stop.

How would you feel if you had to remain in that posture for the next 10 minutes?

Stop.

Where have you observed such an attitude in yourself or others?

(If you want to take notes, now ...)

4.1.6 Posture B

Stand up again so that the weight of your upper body is now resting above the pelvis. No - not that you should sit "straight up." Let the shoulders fall smoothly to their normal, familiar position.

Stop.

Now place your legs in a comfortable parallel position. Where would you like to put your arms down? "In the lap?

Stop.

What do you feel about this attitude?

Stop.

Where have you observed this attitude in yourself or others?

Stop.

If you describe the inner attitude that goes along with this outward attitude: in which attribute list below would you find a word that comes closest to your impression?

First: Anxious / inhibited / insecure / shy / timid.

Second: Open / waiting / attention.

Third: Arrogant / bored / party atmosphere.

(If you want to take notes, now ...)

4.1.7 Sitting Posture C

Now shift the bodyweight backward by leaning against it.

Stop.

What other movements did your body perform automatically?

Stop.

Have you stretched out one or both legs or felt the impulse to roll over a leg? (From which you can see that a signal alone, such as a folded leg, has no significance.) Often one only wants to support the spine, because that depends on how high the chair legs are in relation to the height of the person sitting.) If you want to take notes, now ...)

4.1.8 How Are You?

Now move to a place in the room where you can walk at least 10 paces (better more) and then walk that stretch, trying to feel "how" you are walking.
Stop.
Repeat walking several times until you think you can answer some questions about your gait before you read it (which your gait could affect!).
Stop.
Now   for   the   questions:

1. Where did you find your "center of gravity" (this does not necessarily mean physical weight)? In the head, chest, abdomen, back, buttocks or legs?

2. Do you tend to be more deliberate /hesitant/restrained or do you walk royally or do you run energetically, space-engaging, purposefully?

3. Go around again and try to answer the following questions: How do I go in rooms? And: How do I walk on the street?

Stop.

Could you tell a difference?

(If you want to take notes, now ...)

4.1.9 What Do You Think?

The last questions are about the way you lie down. Here's your memory to answer:

1. How do you lie down when you go to bed?

2. How do you feel about getting ready to fall asleep?

3. In which position do you wake up in the morning?

Stop.

Did you play along before you read on?

If not, consider whether you want to take advantage of this inventory before turning the page?

4.2 External and Internal Posture

When we say of a man that he is steadfast, we not only describe his inner attitude, but we also say something about his type of soil adhesion. LÖWEN, an American psychoanalyst who, as a bio-energetic, deals in particular with the posture, facial expressions, and gestures of his patients:

"The problem of the emotional security of a person cannot be separated from the question of physical security, of his grip on the feet."

Eastern wisdom has also made this observation. In Zen Buddhism, one speaks of man's "center of the earth" as lying in the abdomen (Hara). DÜRKHEIM (22) notes that Westerners have generally shifted their emphasis too high, e.g. in the chest or even in the head. From such a man he says that one can already shake him by the slightest thrust. It is clear that such a person is physically and mentally not "on the ground" so that even minor "puissions" can already unsettle him.

FELDENKRAIS (29) means the same thing when he demands that a body in optimal posture "should hang in the skeleton," he wants to say that no unnecessary muscle work (tension) should be necessary to keep the body standing, walking, or sitting upright. If you think back to the two experiments in which you are so far forward or. have bent back until you almost fell over - you have found that the tension was stronger than usual, but you were quite familiar? The more muscular activity is needed to maintain the posture, the more insecure it is, the more strained it is, i.e. when a person is standing, walking, or sitting relaxed. But since the physical and mental-spiritual processes constantly influence each other, this means at the same time that such a person is emotionally "cramped."

We usually assume that we have a body, whereas the eastern person would never make such a statement (Wats, 87). He says: "I am my body." This sentence reflects the fundamental difference of two contradictory shots, that of being and that of having volition. The stronger the Haben-Wolien orientation is pronounced, the less consciously does man perceive his own being-in-the-world. This also applies to his physical processes and signals! He focuses on things he wants to get hold of. He is looking for things he can handle. This inner attitude will inevitably be reflected in the outer. Lions says (57a):

"Wherever there is fundamental insecurity in the lower half of the body, the individual compensates by holding on to the objective reality with his arms and eyes."

He also describes such a type of person:
"Several years ago, I treated a patient with severe hypertension. He was a press agent for several

Hollywood stars and film producers. He ate too much, was a heavy drinker, and apt to talk. He had a blooming, round face, and a full body. Laying off his clothes, I was shocked by the spindly legs ... coming out. The implication that the apparent security and strength of the upper body compensated for the weakness was inevitable. His main activities were limited to the upper half of the body and essentially oral in nature ."

If a person suffers from disharmony, lack of peace, lack of inner peace, then he does not rest in himself. Then he is not his body, but he "has" one whom he also neglects. Another author, SCHUTZ, has created an excellent cycle of exercises that can be used to both identify and remedy any difficulties with your own posture (internal as well as external) (77). Such an exercise exists in that one on a couch or a mattress beats as strong as possible. What about such exercises is described by LÖWEN, who also uses this exercise in the therapeutic field (57a)?

"Recently I treated a young man, a jet pilot in the navy ...

His problem showed up when I asked him to hit the couch. Every time he took off, his feet lifted off the ground. When I pointed it in any way and noticed how hard it fell to him to maintain contact with the bottom, he said, "Now I know why I feel in the air so much safer" (p 98!)

These were just a few thoughts that one can relate to one's own attitude or the correlation of one's own inner and outer attitude. Whoever is in this would like to deepen an extremely important topic (mentally and physically!), which both the aforementioned book by SCHUTZ (77) and "Hara" by DÜRKHEIM (22) are recommended. In this context, I would like to refer you to the excellent book "The Upright Walk" by FELDENKRAIS (29), which is now available again after it has been out of print for a long time. (All page numbers in FELDENKRAIS quotes refer to the out-of-print issue.)

These three books provide a fascinating overall view and include hands-on exercises - unlike other, certainly readable books that sadly do not. (All three are available in German.) The second reason why I just want to put these three books so warmly to your heart is due to the excellent readability of all three authors. So, and now we want to turn to the signals of others (?!).

4.2.1 About Standing

The first thing we can focus on is weight shifting. Is the human being upright (without being stick-stiff) or is his weight shifted in front of or behind the pelvis? (If in doubt, mentally draw a line up from the pelvis, in a straight-line posture, the ear is approximately on this line, even if the back looks a little crooked).

Now the theory of body language actually says the same thing as the vernacular: the straighter someone stands, the more upright is his inner attitude. Such a person is neither insecure (tilt forward) nor overbearing (tilt backward). Nevertheless, caution is advised: Many especially tall people have adopted a forward-leaning attitude because they do not always want to look down "from above." Similarly, some very small people have learned to take a slightly reclined posture, so they do not always have to look up. Thus, the body posture, as far as the aspect just discussed, can be a signal, but only one. Only when other aspects reinforce the impression, can one assume that one understands the other's signals. One such second aspect that we can look for is the openness or closeness of an attitude. This refers to the cervical and thoracic space. Since time immemorial a creature protects its carotid artery in danger. Man does this by raising his shoulders and/or pulling his head. In some cases, he hides behind his arms or behind an object (e.g. a folder), which he uses as a shield. Surely you know people who almost never cover this area, others who chronically cover it. One runs, carrying a file, open through the company, the other closed.

The opposite of the latter attitude we see in an "overbearing." Here, man signals how safe he feels. Or does he want to achieve this certainty, which he displays so exaggeratedly, perhaps through this attitude? [Personally, I assume that there is no "real" arrogance, but that all aspects of the ostentatious "over-elevating" and "looking-to-see" will always arise out of the need to create insecurity to hide himself and others). That is why such a person often acts "arrogantly" on others (see Introduction and Chapter 1).]

We, therefore, call the straight posture an open one. It signals openness to others and to the world as well as a position from which to re-act in both directions when circumstances require it. So also, a flexible attitude! Now, the attitude is still accompanied by other signals, for example, the way someone looks at us (or not).

The posture A, which we have described as "overbearing," does not work that way until the line of sight simultaneously runs from top to bottom. For then, in the other case, we assume such an "I-up-there-down-feeling" to misuse WALLRAFF's title (86). Interesting to me is the fact that one tends to get annoyed at the overbearing attitude of another. Maybe we should feel sorry for a person who needs to take that attitude. It is the size that you really own and that does not particularly need demonstrating!

Posture B, which we have called "open," is usually accompanied by a straight (open-looking) gaze. So, we do not perceive this signal as negative unless the other one "stares" at us.

Posture C, commonly called the "humility posture," is either accompanied by a view from below or a lack of eye contact. We both feel it, but how do we feel that? There are people who love humility attitudes in others, and there are people who deal with such a thing and the conversation partner does not feel well. Somewhat spitefully, one could say that with some authorities it is advisable to take the humility attitude if one wants to achieve something ...

What we can also pay attention to is whether a person is free or whether he is looking for support somewhere. There are people who always have to lean on something. Others do not make use of the possibilities of leaning on, even if they are present. You can watch this in a bar or at some bars. Again, the vernacular gives us a hint when he says someone needs to lean on. For a person who hangs in his skeleton (FELDENKRAIS 29), who rests in the middle of his earth (DÜRKHEIM 22) or who possesses safety through grip (LÖWEN 27a), will sometimes, but by no means, always want to lean against.

This aspect can be observed especially well with teachers or speakers. (The next parliamentary debate, which is televised, would be a good start!) Some speakers cling to the desk, others seem to "hold on" to their disposition, while others are mostly free. If one or the other pose expresses a habit attitude, then it seems probable that this habitual attitude reflects the inner attitude of the individual.

Another aspect of standing (as well as sitting) is the distance we take to (or from?) others. It can also be interesting to observe how (quietly) someone stands. Does he fidget, does he keep rocking on the balls of his feet or is he stuck on the ground?

Interpretations are based on the lines of thought in 4.2. There are certainly other aspects, but I think that there is less here. If you pay attention to the mentioned aspects of the different categories, you have a frame of reference that will help you. The more one wants to see "at once," the less one realizes in the end. That's why we are now turning to walking.

4.2.2 About Walking

Almost everything that applies to standing, naturally also applies to walking. In addition, however, a walking body is in motion, so one can wonder how he performs that movement. Does a human being go unerringly? Are his movements fluid, supple, agile, or stiff and cramped?

There are authors who think that the gaze of a walking person says a lot about him. So, an outside-directed person looks forward, both the way he wants to go, as well as interesting on the way perceiving. While an interior-oriented person looks more "inward." He has lowered his head and often does not perceive his path or obstacles (nor other people or interesting things).

Signal effects can also have the way a person sets their feet. A person who looks like a "stork in a salad" prefers the knee so that the first point of the body that precedes is, so to speak, the knee. This gait is correlated with caution or uncertainty. A soldier in a minefield will go like this or someone who is afraid to push in the dark.

In contrast, one can also walk so that the toes always precede. This is where the heel is firmly attached, in contrast to the "stork walk" in which the whole foot (focus on the ball of the foot) has to be put on.

A toe gait is therefore usually a strong gait, a room more engaging. So, someone who is not afraid to hurt himself is running. Someone with a clear goal in mind, someone in a hurry. Excellent observation points are marketplaces, railway stations, church exits after the service, as well as main roads at peak times.

Walking in pairs or more can also be instructive. Some authors argue that empathy and selfishness are expressed in the way someone walks with one (or more) person (s). Does he care if he runs too fast or too slow for others? Does he even notice when others are far behind because they do not come along? Is it necessary to repeatedly ask him to be considerate?

Of course, another aspect of walking to several can also be distance. However, since we spend most of our time sitting down with other people, interpretations are more applicable.

4.2.3 About Sitting

Again, our first look should be focused on whether the body weight is in front, above or behind the pelvis.

Let's start with attitude A, the so-called escape position. Do you remember still on your seat experiments? This attitude is taken when one feels uncomfortable or insecure. In the waiting room of a dentist, you often see that.

Since the body weight is in front of the pelvis, you can get up very quickly and walk away (run away).

Especially if the feet are in step position. If a conversation partner you are dealing with takes this attitude, then do not continue the conversation until you either learn the reason for the attitude or change the other's attitude with help from you. A person who sits like this is in a position of flight, also internally. That is, he u. U. now produces stress hormones and that his "reptilian brain" cooperates. So, you cannot count on his "brain of thought" working very well at the moment. After FESTINGER (31), we speak of the psychological fog.

Now, although we said that a signal alone is usually meaningless, we indicated that there would be exceptions to this rule. Sitting posture can be such an exception, especially if it is suddenly changed. For example, when a person suddenly moves to the escape position. This situation is described by another rule:

Any sudden change in outward attitude always reflects a sudden change in the inner attitude.

This should also be very plausible given the information given in 4.2. When you did the little experiment cycle, even in these brief moments when you have taken individual postures, you could already see that every posture of the body is influencing the inner posture (and vice versa)!

Although the above description shows that the escape situation can be interpreted quite reliably, one should not forget the control question. Someone may have back pain and bends forward, to relieve some muscle parts? Maybe he also goes to the escape position because he wants to go to the bathroom and waits for a favorable moment because he does not want to interrupt the others? (Especially if he's sitting so that maybe someone has to get up to let him through?)

Posture B shows again our flexible, open posture. A human being like that is ready to take on the environment or to respond to it. It is a wait-and-see or attentive attitude. That's why in the early days, school was so important that we sat upright on the bench, our hands on the desk, our eyes straight ahead. This body posture also causes inner openness and shows that whatever the external stimulus is, it is really respected.

As long as your interlocutor is in such a position, you can generally assume that he is taking your messages or is interested in the conversation or in you. (Which does not mean that interest cannot exist in other postures, only: This attitude can be used as a signal for Interest to be interpreted.)

At this point, the seminar always raises a question: "How can one distinguish the position of escape from prevention of interest?." An excellent question, don't you think?

Your answer has to do with the line of sight. In the escape position, the head is inclined downwards, so that (parallel to the humility in standing position) the view is directed from bottom to top, if at all eye contact comes about. A sudden self-interest prevention, however, is accompanied by a straight head, that is, a straight, open (interested) gaze.

This repeated anticipation of facial expressions clearly shows two things: First, what we mean when we say that as a rule, a signal alone has no significance. The connection of the various signals to "sentences" can be interpreted, but not individual "words" (exceptions only confirm the rule). Secondly, you see how important the signals of facial expressions in association with other signals are!

Posture B can now be more or less open. It can be someone right now sit, but still, partially cover the chest and neck (e.g. by a supporting arm and a hand on the mouth). Again, we see that signals of the gestures (the distance, as well as the tone) must be taken into account before we can interpret anything.

The attitude C corresponds to the overbearing attitude while standing, as the bodyweight is shifted to the rear. Right? Not correct! Although here the weight of the upper body is stored backward, we cannot draw this correlation. Why? Think with! When does one sit far back, perhaps overturn one leg or even put up both feet?

Right. If you want to make yourself comfortable. Here it is interesting that some people like to "cuddle," while others prefer an upright, straight attitude even in the private sphere, during sociable hours, watching TV, reading, etc. So, you cannot say, this tilted back seats usually express an arrogance.

Again, we see how careful we have to be in the interpretation. In order to increase the confusion, I allow myself to conclude that the attitude C can very well mean arrogance. The emphasis is on "can." That's why it's so important to always look at several signals in the bandage as well as to assess the signals in conjunction with the words, and of course to determine by control questions whether we guessed or "interpreted" it rightly.

I once had a seminar participant, who had already noticed me standing around the seminar, by his leaning back posture, his view from above (coupled with a certain pull around the mouth, a constant slight lifting of the eyebrows and other signals, which we will discuss later). But I could not ask a control question. ("Are you arrogant, sir?")

Now I was curious about what impressions I would gather in the course of the seminar, which would either confirm or falsify the "arrogant" interpretation. What do you think? For four days, man tilted his chair back against the wall, so that he could still keep his "view from above" while seated. Whether he really wanted it or not is not certain. But surely, I know that the whole group found him arrogant. He himself told me (in private) that he is always an outsider wherever he goes. Does it surprise you?

All previous information can help us, especially when it comes to perceiving sudden changes in posture while sitting. Try this: sit back and lean forward, then jerk your upper body forward. Repeat this movement ten times. Then, find out how much power you need!

Now our organism is extremely economical. He wastes no unnecessary power. You can run energetically and purposefully, but you cannot walk energetically (say with great effort). As long as a person is internally in a position that could be called a "mental stroll," he will not spend much energy, unless ... you guessed it? Unless, of course, something had suddenly caught his attention and caused him to turn to that something energetically. (Conversely, one can abruptly lose his interest and let himself fall into the state of "psychic learning," for example, by letting himself fall back into the pillows.) An example:

Suppose you are at a party. Your interlocutor sits (you could almost say: lying) comfortably leaning back in a pronounced C-posture. He tells you so casually that he plans to sell his second car soon, as his daughter, who drove him so far, emigrated to Australia. They also casually ask what kind of car it is and they now find out that it is a car that would interest you, as you may, for example, currently looking for a second car. Their limit is, say, 2000 marks and you know that you have to take your time doing something good for this money. Of course, you expect your partner to want more for his car, but ask him anyway. Suppose he says, "I do not know yet? Why, are you interested? "His attitude has still not changed because he does not (yet) believe that he is talking to a potential buyer. They say vaguely, "Maybe?," To which he says, "What would you offer?" And now the following happens: They say, "About 2000 marks." He leans forward abruptly, claiming "far too little." What do you conclude from his sudden shift in body weight, from a "soul-wandering" attitude to an upright-looking, very loving one?

If you believed his words, you would probably have missed the chance! Here we have an incongruence, similar to the case of NIXON (see Introduction).

Another case study on the sudden shift in weight: In 1974, I wrote a body language article for a magazine. The editor-in-chief sat in a huge editor-in-chief, leaning back, relaxed, and looking down at my manuscript, which he was half bored, half interested. When he came to the description of the sitting posture, he looked at me over the edge of the manuscript and said, "That's nice, what's written here, but scientifically that's nonsense, isn't it?"

"No, no, not at all," I said about the huge editor desk sitting right up to him, "certain studies have clearly shown ..."

"What studies?" He asked, suddenly upright and interested in prevention.

"How are you sitting there now?" I laughed.

"Pure coincidence, sheer coincidence," he replied, leaning back again.

(I lured him twice more to the edge of the chair before he realized that certain basic processes such as body weight shifting are not just "gray theory.")

4.2.4 NN Contact (After Susmann)

As far as the posture is concerned, another criterion can be used for the assessment. However, this only applies to longer conversations. It is a signal that contains less of a message, but rather an inner attitude. A colleague, Dr. Ing. Franz SUSMANN coined the beautiful word "NN-Kontakt" for the description. The point is that the theory says that the thorax of a person says doubt about the real interest more than the eyes of the two do not point in one direction. NN stands for "nose" and "navel," a very memorable expression. In groups, you can observe that participants or group leaders (including bosses), which are accepted and respected by the group, get in a longer statement not only the eyes (noses) but also the breasts (navel) facing the group members. Other participants (or bosses) must be happy when the pairs of eyes are pointed at them, others are not even looked at. Mind you - in a lively discussion where each speaker speaks for less than two minutes, one cannot expect all participants to turn their bodies around! But in situations where the individual speaker speaks (or lectures) for more than 15 minutes, this signal becomes quite meaningful. Also, in this aspect, it pays to take care at the next parliamentary debate once, when the camera detects the more or less inclined audience. Some read or talk to their neighbors, so they do not turn their nose or navel over to the speaker. Others sit sideways, with their arm resting on the back of the neighbor as they turn their faces (not always their eyes) forward, etc.

But this behavior changes from time to time, namely, when the speaker is in front, who knows how to address. (Unfortunately, these are only a few!)

4.2.5 About Lying Down

Have you ever wondered if your sleeping posture could send a signal? What do you mean by someone who pulls himself together like a ball of yarn or someone who "dominates" the bed so widely that no one else has room next to him? Do you think that a belly or Supine position can say something about the sleeper?

Well, an American psychiatrist, Samuel DUNKELL, believes that. In his book "Body Language in Sleep" (24), he laments the fact that, despite the more than 600 papers published annually on sleep, virtually nothing is said about sleep positions Although the first timid approaches in this direction are already decades old. However, this also means that at present there is almost only his own approach. It is to be hoped that kineticists will soon take on this topic as well. Although the work of an individual will still be considered with caution, it is worth m. E. but to deal with her. I find some of his conclusions very plausible. When he thinks

"That a close connection between the sleeping positions of people and other factors known about him exists. That is, the posture that gives a person such a sense of security that he takes them in the sleeping world is for his way of life... revealing. "

About people who in the fetus position (completely rolled up, an absolutely closed posture) sleep, he says:

"Such people in the daytime world (as in the night) show a strong need for protection and the desire for a center, a core around which they can build their lives and on which they can learn."
About the sleeper stretched out on the stomach:

"Even when he is awake, he is under the pressure to determine the course of events, his (his) daily environment. (He) does not value surprises ... "

And after sleeping on his back ("royal supine position") he says,

"That they feel as the king or queen of sleep and beyond their whole day universe ... Back sleepers are generally characterized by a ... sense of security, self-confidence and such a strong personality that it is easy for them, the world and its offers to accept."

A 1909 study (Harvard University) showed, as DUNKELL mentions, that 75% of the subjects who slept in the so-called semi-fetal position. This sleeping position is a lateral position with slightly tightened knees:

"It has the advantage that the heat is stored and the air can freely circulate around the body. In addition, the main parts of the trunk, especially the psychological center, the heart, are protected. In addition, the semi-fetal posture offers greater flexibility than the other common body postures, as the sleeper - without having to change the usual sleeping position - turns from one side to the other can ... The situation is therefore not only comfortable but also expedient, in one word pronouncedly

»reasonable." Correspondingly, the people who prefer them have adapted to the world. By and large, they are well-balanced, self-assured people who understand the facts without any particular psychological stress ... "

I think that thinking about our sleeping positions is well worthwhile, even if we do not agree with Dunkell's statements on every point. Because there must be a connection between our day and night posture, since we are our bodies - even in sleep - seems safe. Moreover, since body language is sometimes "unconsciously" spoken unconsciously, the nocturnal "unconscious language" must also have meaningfulness. The question remains, how "good" can one interpret it, provided one dares to try it!

At the end of the section on the posture, I would like to point out once again that signal groups can give the most meaning. Therefore, the previous information usually only in association with the signals, which we will discuss, to understand as body language news.

Image by Jonathan Alvarez

Are you familiar with your facial expressions? Do you really say with your face what you want to express with your words???

Now ...look at yourself in the mirror....and
try to express these feelings with your face:

Fear, Joy,
Sympathy, Fatigue,
Energy, Curiosity....

........and many others!!!

Repeat test after reading the following
chapter

Chapter 5: Facial Expressions

5.1 Facial Expressions and Physiognomy

As we already mentioned in Chapter 2, we want to understand by facial expressions all phenomena that we can observe in the face of a human being. By this, we mean both facial features, eye contact, and viewing direction, as well as psychosomatic processes, such as pale. Finally, we also include entire head movements with, such. As a nodding, oblique (the latter, depending on the context, of course, the attitude can be assigned).

In general, we are concerned with the evaluation of congruence signals. As long as the facial expressions match the verbal utterances, we usually do not take them very well. When the incongruity is strong, it attracts even the most inexperienced. But the experienced can take note of a variety of facial expressions in order to perceive even slight disturbances or incipient incongruence (or, of course, first signs of relief, approval, etc.). Often only a barely perceptible grin indicates that someone is making a joke. Or it may be that a (questioning) raised eyebrow is the only indication of incongruity when the other one says, "Yes, I understand exactly what you mean."

At this point in the seminar, the question often arises of how far one can manipulate his non-linguistic signals. To what extent z. For example, it would be possible not to let it be noted whether one grasps or approves of something?
Answer: Of course, anyone can learn to influence his body language to a degree.

However, it is particularly difficult to get the facial muscles under control. So, you can often observe that someone looks outwardly calm because he has learned to control his hands (for example, by intertwining his fingers to prevent him from playing around nervously). Nevertheless, an inner restlessness (if any) will express itself, and most likely in the face. Why is the manipulation of our facial muscles so difficult? The word "manipulate" includes the word manus (lat., The hand). However, to be able to handle something skillfully, you have to know it well. We do not know enough about our facial muscles to get a grip on them. In general, we do not know how we look or how we affect others. Try it (right now) yourself! Check your own facial expression ...

A real experiment on this would look like this: You get a small pocket mirror, which you always have at hand in the near future. Now and then you will try to first feel your expression, and then immediately to see in the mirror. Ask yourself before and while you look in each case: "How do I look now? How do I now seem to others?" (Or how would I act on others now?)

You will experience very exciting surprises, although they are not positively fascinating for everyone. Some people are horrified when they realize how often they have a discontented, disgruntled look around their mouths and eyes that they did not even realize! However, the less you know about his facial expression, the less you really know him, the less you can of course also manipulate him, that is, you have it.

A second mini-experiment that you can do immediately confirms this. After reading the instruction, close your eyes briefly and try to relax your face, especially the lips and chin, as much as possible. Observe and feel consciously what it feels like.

Stop.

Now three questions:

- Have you achieved relaxation?

- Have you got a feel for feeling your own facial muscles?

- Were your lips laid together loosely?

If you answered yes to the last question, then you have confirmed what FELDENKRAIS (29) means when he says:

"How is it that such an important part of the body as the lower jaw is constantly held up? Muscles that work uninterruptedly while we are awake, without even the slightest sensation that we are doing something to hold the jaw up?

To drop it, you even have to learn how to apply the muscle inhibitor. If one tries to relax his lower jaw so much that he falls through his own weight and opens his mouth completely, so you will wonder how difficult that is. If it finally succeeds, one will notice changes in the facial expression and in the eyes. It will probably also be noticed later that one usually presses his lower jaw upwards or keeps his mouth firmly closed. "

Did the little experiments teach you a little about how little you normally know about your facial muscles? Every actor who deals (or mainly) with pantomime knows the difficulties associated with the conscious creation of a desired facial expression.

The knowledge of the difficulties of manipulating one's facial expressions is not only important if we want to control our own facial expressions (with too much control, if they succeed, resulting in a robotic, non-living expression!) but the Information is also essential if we want to interpret the signals of others. Since the other person is just as unaware of his facial expressions, one can rely on the facial expressions in general quite well.

By the way, the study of the facial expression is divided into two areas, the facial expression itself and the physiognomy. Under the latter one understands not the momentary, ever-changing expression, but the facial features that a person has in general. I call that the "facial expression." If a person often expresses displeasure by squeezing his lips and lowering the corners of his mouth, then it does not surprise him if he has so-called mis-wrinkles after years. These are deeply scored "lines" that run down from the corners of the mouth. Anyone who looks at the face of the young SCHOPENHAUER and then compares it with the image of the old can clearly see this (see also: "the compressed mouth").

The physiognomy also includes an interpretation of the facial or nasal form, although here the separation from the phrenology which GALL (94) founded is not clear. We will not practice physiognomy or phrenology.

Nevertheless, we can not help but for example, to register deep scored wrinkles when we consciously perceive. But even such a signal alone has no significance. To be sure, the wrinkling itself is unmistakable, so that we know that this man must often have his lips pinched and the corners of his mouth lowered, but we do not know why this happened. Of course, it may be that this human being is a "Griesgram" who does not like anything. But it may just as well be that this person has suffered a serious illness or a hard fate. Think of persons who have lost a loved one, to people who have spent years in concentration camps or to those who have been tortured (as is commonplace in certain parts of the world today), etc.

It has become customary to assume the following subdivision:

1. Forehead area (including the eyebrows)

2. Midface, i.e.: eye, nose, and cheek area (for most authors including the upper lip)

3. Mouth (or lower lip) and chin area.

5.1.1 The Forehead Area

It is believed that the forehead, with its wrinkles and eyebrows, provides information about processes of thinking and analyzing. Although this opinion seems to be a remnant of the phrenology of GALL (94), I still hold the statements on the forehead applicable. Nevertheless, of course, there is the demand for caution on the part of "scientificity" of such interpretations.

5.1.2 The Midface

The eye, nose, and cheek area is also referred to as the sense of sight. Most authors include the upper lip because they make more nuanced detail statements than we do. We usually only speak of the Lips or from the mouth, so that it is not so important in our frame, where you want to draw the border exactly.

The sense of sight is said to give us clues about taking on the outside world. This is because the eyes are the "window to the world." But they are rightly called the "window to the soul," so that we see that information from the inner life can also be seen in this area. It should also be borne in mind that the mouth also plays a key role in the processes of environmental uptake.

5.1.3 The Mouth and Chin Area

The mouth has developed from the Ur-Maw, which already has a very simple organism. It represents the relationship to the environment, in that the organism absorbs as well as eliminates it. In small children, it is easy to see that they put everything in their mouths to grasp it. Therefore, it is not surprising that the mouth plays an essential role, both when it comes to not "let in" information from the environment and when one does not want to or is not allowed to express.

Next assign the chin part (including the lower lip) the emotional and instinctive life, and, especially the chin, the assertiveness. A person who is about to assert himself vigorously will push his chin as a mimic signal. (While the assessment of the chin shape regarding the character traits of assertiveness belongs to the field of phrenology.)

And now let's look at the interpretations of the three facial area turns.

5.2 The Forehead Area (Interpretation)

Since we do not want to analyze the shape of the forehead, we are concerned with the mimic expressions of forehead wrinkles, which can be horizontal and/or vertical. Usually, horizontal wrinkles are accompanied by lifting of the eyebrows. But there is also a barely noticeable lifting of one or both brows, which does not wrinkle.

5.2.1 Horizontal Forehead Wrinkles

As a rule of thumb, we can say that the horizontal forehead wrinkles indicate that the attention has been drawn heavily. However, this strong attention can have very different occasions. For example, Zeddies (94) calls the following:

1. Fright

2. Anxiety

3. Obtuseness

4. Astonish

5. Amazement

6. Confusion

7. Surprise

Again, it becomes clear that individual signals (usually) must be seen in association with others. This also applies within a category, such as facial expressions. For the forehead wrinkles are automatically associated with other muscle movements of the face, which then open eyes (or an open mouth) can lead. Such a combination provides, for example, the following:

Horizontal wrinkles and open eyes. According to ZEDDIES (94), the two mean signals interpreted together: "The mental attitude lies in a waiting, attentive attitude to any circumstances that offer themselves to the consciousness."

Another combination possibility of two mimic signals would be the formation of horizontal forehead wrinkles in conjunction with half-closed (= easy squinted) eyes. This combination can be observed if someone goes to great lengths to listen; in the case of the hard of hearing, for example, or in situations in which the volume of the transmitter (including technical sound sources such as a radio) is not sufficient. The vernacular describes this with the expression "the ears are pointed." However, this formulation not only describes "in a figurative sense," but also indicates physiological processes. In fact, when we tip our ears, we actually move our severely stunted ear muscles in a reflex that is pronounced in dogs, cats, and rabbits. Often the effort to "play" our "spoons" will be accompanied by an additional gesture and/or attitude change.

The former is to place a hand on the pinna to enlarge and direct it forward. (This is exactly like the sharpened, erect dog ear.) The latter consists of a turning to the "sound source," for example to the speaker, whom one would like to understand better. However, one can observe this turning even with mechanical sound sources such as a TV set.

Since it would be beyond the scope of our necessarily very crude analysis to list all possible combinations of two or more signals (which, depending on accuracy, would take 600-60,000 pages), we will confine ourselves to simple signals. The above examples should only give some idea of how detailed even "rough" scientific investigations can be.

You learn most about the forehead region as you learn to consciously register the primary (= primary) signals, while at the same time you develop an unconscious sense of the secondary features through regular exercise. The easiest way to do this is to become a scientist and learn to elicit signals that you want to study in others! The other one can be told afterward that you have used it as a "guinea pig" (forgiveness, as a subject), or not if you act skillfully. One option for targeted observation is the following experiment that you should do as often as possible.

5.2.2 An Experiment for Horizontal Wrinkling

They get a cassette (a tape recorder) with a foreign-language text, prose, or even songs. According to the motto "do you speak English?" You are looking for someone who knows this foreign language "quite well"

, but not fluently. Now ask that person to help you understand your cassette text. Then you play your recording, lean back comfortably, and observe the (more or less pronounced) formation of horizontal wrinkles on the forehead. First, you will usually see a slight lifting of the eyebrows ...

You now consciously register only the forehead signals, but unconsciously store a variety of secondary impressions such as Mouth and/or eye signals associated with those of the forehead.

The more often you perform this experiment, the more likely you are to develop a good sense of how easy or difficult it is for someone to understand you if you want to explain something! How often do we tell a person something, stringing together ten, a hundred, or more units of information known to us, even though these messages are for our addressee, and so on? You could include too many new things in one approach.

In particular, I would like to recommend this training to all persons who are entrusted with the education or training of fellow human beings. Apprentices in industry, students, new employees, and countless children would appreciate it if more people knew how to interpret this signal group better! Because often one does not dare to interrupt to inquire. Sometimes it is embarrassing to admit before the other person or the group around you that you do not understand everything.

5.2.3 Vertical Forehead Wrinkles

We said that the horizontal folds indicate that the attention is being drawn heavily. As far as the vertical folds are concerned, the following sentence applies:

Vertical forehead wrinkles indicate that all attention is focused on something (someone).

So, if you're the previously previous experiments have been tried, then it may well be that you have also seen vertical wrinkles. As with the horizontal ones, there are different possibilities. Concentration always means "contracting." This can mean both mental and physical strength combined at one point so that we can register vertical forehead wrinkles both in mental concentration and in difficult, complicated, or strenuous physical activities. Likewise, it can be seen that determination as a secondary feature has such wrinkles, while the primary features will be in the mouth and chin area. Anger or disgusting irritation can also be a cause for the formation of vertical wrinkles. Even when "naserümpfen" can arise as a secondary feature wrinkling.

For this reason, what has been said under 5.3.2 also applies: Only the deliberate observation and conscious registration of the forehead wrinkles (by repeated practice) leads to a simultaneous perception of the remaining signals. Again, this one Experiment, which is ideal as a beer table or coffee round gag.

5.2.4 An Experiment for Vertical Wrinkling

You ask the group:

"Who can get a match out of a box with one hand and set it alight without putting the box on the table or anywhere else?"

Anyone who makes this attempt will, to your delight, form into weaker or stronger vertical forehead wrinkles! Again, this practice, if often done daily, brings you benefits: An initial eyebrow contraction, which precedes vertical wrinkling (or represents a weaker signal of equal importance), can give you a valuable clue when you give something to someone want to disassemble. This signal means concentration. If your counterpart sees it while looking at you at the same time, it most likely focuses on the content of your words. However, if your caller sends this signal while looking at you (i.e. away from you), then this may be. It may mean that he wants to rethink something you just said (see chapter 5.4). Maybe questions or doubts have surfaced with him?

Maybe he imagines applications of your proposal? Here is a control question of the third kind, so an active silence, the best. However, here we have an exception to the rule that others mostly speak into silence: if the observed signals have indicated that your counterpart is thinking, thinking carefully, it may well be that at first it does not notice your silence. It takes a few moments for a thoughtful person to realize that a noise1 is suddenly gone. Everyone can remember moments in school as the teacher watched a classmate distract, stop talking, looked at the unlucky fellow who for a few moments did not know he had all the (amused) attention of everyone! In this context, I always have to remember Mark Twain's Tom Sawyer playing with his bench mate by crawling a small beetle on the slate and collecting points as the beast went one way or another until the entire class fascinated watched the teacher finish the game...

5.2.5 Movement of The Eyebrows

Much of all eyebrow movement is related or in preparation for wrinkling. However, if only the brow(s) lifts (lift), then this approach is already a signal towards those wrinkling be emitted more pronounced. Furthermore, we can only proceed in a simplistic way within this framework. Therefore, we will not perform a detailed analysis of possible displacements of half a millimeter, although this may be a fascinating undertaking. You also learn most about eyebrows through targeted observation. A mini-experiment on this: Observe once the eyebrows of a person, you (intentionally) address by name, but slightly change it.

They are unmotivated gestures that have

motivations.

(Andrea Pinketts)

5.3 The Middle Face (Interpretation)

Let's start with the eye. After all, man is not unjustly called an "eye animal" because he takes in more than 80% of all stimuli through the eyes. At least this is the "scientific" opinion, some researchers even set the percentage to over ninety.

As already mentioned, the eye can be described both as a "window to the world" and as a "window to the soul," that is, to intrapsychic processes. The latter processes, however, are closely related to the private thinking processes and emotional processes of man. Therefore, information about this in our context should not be discussed in detail. We do not want to operate or approach telepathy, but outward-looking better understand the signals that are constantly being transmitted. Therefore, we will pay more attention to these signals, or only to those interior-facing people who want to take on the environment or a current non-recording desire.

5.3.1 The Definite, Firm, Open View

Many people believe that a definite, fixed gaze should go hand in hand with an immobile pupil, as opposed to the "restless" gaze. But that's not true, because a "fixed" view is always an "unsteady" one. Think about it: If you remember the last time you looked really hard into someone's eyes (remember it?) ... you looked that person in the eyes, not in the eye. That is, your gaze kept moving from one eye to the other! If your last such experience was so long ago that you cannot imagine this process at the moment, go to the mirror and try "eye contact" with yourself! Stop.

Do you have a clear picture of this process in your mind's eye? Then you understand that a firm look must be a moving one! If one were to really see someone else firmly in the eye (i.e. to fix him), then the feeling that was triggered by it would be a most alienating one.

Therefore, it is not surprising that one feels uncomfortable in the presence of some people who have "learned" and trained eye contact in an exaggerated form. If you for example, if you have the opportunity to speak with members of the Church of Scientology (also known as Dianetics), which is also in Germany, then you can watch this constant stare. If this is then accompanied by a frozen light "smile," as "masters" of the system understand it to "radiate," then the impression of having to deal with a robotic-programmed, depersonalized "person" becomes even stronger. Similar observations can also be made with American graduates of several "est courses," as well as with the followers of many juvenile sects, also with participants of some so-called rhetoric seminars!

Let us, therefore, hold that a "steady" gaze is also more alive. As all life pulsates, so does the pupil constantly to (fractions of a) millimeter (s) back and forth.

5.3.2 Eye Contact

As a rule, I would like to put the following sentence in the room:

Eye contact is called eye contact because it creates contact.

Now, eye contact can also avoid this contact, although he seems to be looking for him. This is the case when one stares at someone (as in the examples above). A rule of some rhetoric and communication coach states. For example, one should see the other firmly and definitely on the root of the nose. This cannot promote genuine, warm, understanding contact, but must be strange! In addition, the pupil movements when stared at a spot are so minimal that they can hardly be perceived by the naked eye. While a lively look, in which one "wanders" from pupil to pupil, is the kind of gaze we mean by eye contact!

Now the theory says that the eye is an excellent indicator of interest. But please do not forget that it can only be an indicator because also the chest cavity, as well as the mouth (see below), play an essential role here.

In eye contact, we can, therefore, assume that the communication is "good." But what about when eye contact is avoided? First an experiment again: Have a conversation with someone in the near future, in which you will tell each other something. If you could quickly chat with a neighbor or colleague before you read on, it would be optimal. They will pay attention to eye contact and try to determine what "good" eye contact is.
Stop.
If you had the opportunity to try this, you may have already noticed the following statement:

Contrary to popular belief, "good" eye contact is not constant. Instead, we understand by "good" eye contact that the listener (almost) constantly looks at the, while the speaker looks at the listener less frequently. This is related to the fact that we cannot simultaneously think intensely and perceive information that is irrelevant to this process of thought. Therefore, a reflection often looks up at the ceiling (as if it were written there) or sideways away or down. This look is not really a look, because he is not consciously aware right now. He "looks inward," or "sinks in thought."

The more someone has to think or want what he wants to say, the more likely he is to interrupt eye contact! You can also test this again specifically.

5.3.3 Eye Contact Experiment

Ask a person a question that you can expect to see have to think about it. For example, what did you do the day before yesterday? Or: When were you last in the cinema? Or: Can you spell "Nuremberg" backward?

Here, you will find that most people in your introduction look away while thinking and beginning to speak. Only at the last words (or after that), the person looks back to you.

On the other hand, like every listener who maintains good eye contact, you have looked at your counterpart all the time so that your counterpart with small control glances can always catch your attention!

5.3.4 Two More Experiments!

Try to think about each statement for about ten minutes in a conversation before you announce it! You will notice that this seems impossible!

Then ask other people to try the same and talk about the difficulties you experience.

As a second experiment, you can try the following: a person who is speaking to you Over the shoulder of!

You will notice that the speaker registers this out of the corner of his eye, even if he did not look directly at you. He will pause, maybe even look around, to see what has drawn your attention!

That is, although we often look away as we think, we can pick up a lot of signals out of the corner of our eyes or when we are sensitive. But there are also people who do not notice this, so they continue to talk "stubbornly," no matter what signals their environment is trying to desperately send them if they do not want to interrupt directly.

These two experiments will both increase your receptivity and be of great value in relation to what has been said below.

5.3.5 Eye Contact as A Strategy?

Although I strongly advise against the idea of "eye contact"

To use "strategy" as this will inevitably lead to excesses as described in 5.4.1, I would like to refer to the following rule:

Eye contact in the sense of control views represents an essential aspect of successful interviewing.

The emphasis is on "one essential aspect." On the one hand, the description of the experiment (see Section 5.4.3) you have shown a possibility that includes the brief control view. On the other hand, it is a fact that one often looks away while thinking. This brings us to a sin in negotiations, which unfortunately happens all too often:

Do you remember our party talk example, in which you were interested in the car of your counterpart (see chapter 4.2.3)? If we want to look at this situation as an example of a negotiation, then an important indication was his suddenly changing posture! After quoting the price we can pay for, he suddenly turned to us (shifting his body weight abruptly), claiming "far too little."

Now imagine that you had to think about your price offer. Then you might have looked at the ceiling and calculated what the car, according to his explanation, includes everything. You might have thought, "He says the tires are new, a stereo is included ...." Imagine, you would have made your price offer still without eye contact. Then it would have been possible for him to sit back again until you looked again. That means you have the most important clue for your Price strategy!

People who are shy, or who seem to avoid eye contact. Here we often react wrongly by asking ourselves to feel uncomfortable and look away as well. Think about it: If you cannot look at the others for any reason, then this does not automatically mean that you do not want to be seen! If you look at him, of course not stare "firmly," possibly with a hint of a frown!), then his small, occasionally used control

glances will show him that he is not "overlooked,"
disregarded, not taken seriously, etc.

Incidentally, I am always asked this point in the
seminar: "Yes, but what about a counterpart who
squints or stutters or is somehow crippled?"

Answer: The cross-eyed person already has enough
problems if squinting (as is often the case) is
accompanied by a (partial) obstruction of vision.
Why should we punish him? by preventing that he
can be viewed? In addition, a person suffers with
something affliction is mainly due to the fact that his
fellow human beings never let him forget that he is
"different" or "handicapped"! Our tendency to look
away here is out of our own discomfort, not because
we want to "help" the other, as verbally gladly
claimed.

As for a man who stutters: Without going into the
psychoanalytic and other theories offered here, we
can say globally that most stutterers do not have a

physiological defect that this way of speaking enforces. So, there is only the possibility of a "psychological" reason. Whatever this may look like (the theories differ here), the effect that is achieved is always the same: the stuttering human being forces his environment to pay more attention to him than a non-stuttering one. You have to concentrate more to understand it.

Incidentally, the same also applies to extremely quiet or unclearly speaking (e.g. mumbling) fellow human beings!

At first, the seminar participants claim that it makes people nervous when they look at them. But that's not true! Rather, it is true that these people are nervous (rightly), if you constantly look on the Mouth, what many listeners do automatically and unconsciously! You too would become nervous if someone constantly sees you on the mouth! Like everyone else, with whom you want to try this once! But that does not mean that we cannot look this person in the eye or should! It is this signal of eye contact that will improve your contact with someone, not avoiding it because you are embarrassed!

5.3.6 Pupil Size as A Signal?

As people have observed, a person whose pupil is contracted acts differently on us than someone whose pupil is wide open. The former view is called piercing. It is said of someone that he had "pig's eye" and so on. The latter is often perceived as an "open eye," though the eyelid itself may not really be very open. Short-sighted people have "beautiful" eyes, as the pupil is larger in order to compensate for the poorer vision. From this, it follows already that an extremely well-sighted person may, therefore, have a rather "piercing" look. Furthermore, it must be remembered that the lighting conditions absolutely must remain the same, if you want to interpret current pupil dilations as interest, or constrictions as disinterest!

In addition, we generally have too little "feeling" for how large a pupil "right now" should be in order to be able to periodically evaluate pupil size as signals from time to time. "Lethich" could be a constriction

(If all the conditions of observation have been fulfilled!) Although this means disinterest, but: We have seen that a person who wants to "process" the information just heard, "sinks into thought," which process also coincides with a narrowing of the pupil accompanied! It's as if he meant to say, "For the moment, please no more Data, before I could think about the given. "This process indicates strong interest, because if not so acute interest he could us continue to talk without sending "shielding" signals of any kind.

From this, we can see how "exact" information is as follows: "Ask your partner if he loves you and pay attention to his answer to the size of his pupil."

5.3.7 The Eye Muscles

As already indicated, there are two parts of the eye, which we can observe: On the one hand the pupil, on the other hand, the total or movements of the eyelids.

So, one speaks from the "imposed" eye, when the upper lid is lowered. This view is accompanied by a limitation of perception. It may be temporary (a fraction of a second) or longer (several minutes). Again, many authors interpret "disinterest" here (see Section 5.4.2).

Even more shielding than the "imposed" effect is the "hidden" eye, in which the upper lid is almost closed. Even with "squinted" eyes, we obscure the sensory organ with which we see, for in mistrust, in reflection, in aggression; at moments when we do not want to see much! However, what we have said now for forehead wrinkling applies even more to the eye: there are always several muscles moving in association with each other. Eyelid movements are associated with both eyebrow movements (forehead area), as well as movements of the mouth muscles! Therefore, the rule that one should learn, the register primary signals of the eyes with these secondary features, the former conscious, the latter simultaneously, but unconsciously.

 Ask someone to tell you something. His presentation should take a little longer, so several minutes. Questions like "How was it on vacation?" Or stories about a movie you're watching are great. Now the person has been asked for the information so that it (unconsciously) starts from the assumption that one will look at it during (attentive) listening. But you do not do that! Even if the person himself hardly looks at you because they are thinking (see above), they will notice in small checks that there is no eye contact. This feels like an incongruent signal from us! Immediately, she will interrupt or ask, " what is?" Or something similar. Now assure "Keep talking."

In hindsight, the person is usually unsettled or upset (rightly so).

So please do not exaggerate!

Nevertheless, such attempts train our eyes enormously, since we determined to induce signals deliberately and not to wait for seeing-practicing until they Eventually come up at random!
Although we have already filled pages with the review of the gaze, we have not yet discussed a fraction of the possible information. But here too it applies that less is more. If you learn to pay attention to the mentioned aspects, then you as a student already see much more than before!

Technically, the midface also includes the nose, as well as the cheek area (and of course the ears). But since the mimic possibilities of nose and ears are minimal, we will not address them here separately. The same applies to the cheek area, although I would like to point out that a relaxed person in the cheek area works differently than a tense one!
As the last information note:

You cannot relax the eye area as long as the mouth is cramped, and vice versa!

Sex is also a form of communication, a way of saying

or demonstrating something that words cannot express just as effectively. "

(Robert Nozick)

5.4 The mouth and the chin (interpretation)

It may not be surprising to observe that an acute desire to seek is often associated with a partially or fully opened mouth. (Even when amazed, the mouth opens.) Conversely, one can observe how the lips close off if one does not want to perceive. The already mentioned disapproving move around the mouth is a good example of this.

Now a compressed mouth can also point out that one does not want to leave "out"1, z. For example, if someone does not want to or is not allowed to express themselves or if someone is afraid to divulge a secret or if someone "bites their lips" so that a thought cannot "slip out."

If you perform the two forehead creasing experiments, you will perceive the mouth as a secondary feature. By contrast, if you pay attention to the position of the mouth, the eyes and/or forehead signals belong to the mimic secondary features.

Our vertical forehead pleat experiment will always include the subject's mouth as well. So that you can practice even more and have more "ammunition" for the same subjects, here's an experiment that you want to pay attention to:

5.4.1 An Oral Distraction Experiment

If we have to make an effort, we often close our mouths. Some stick their tongues out; others stop their mouths (often even in a crooked position). You want to pay attention to this when you choose your group

Ask friends at the beer or coffee table for the next try: Place three coins on your flat hand and show them to the group with these words: "Who can hold these three coins in his hand while taking the middle coin out of the pile and push down without raising your hand or coins somewhere? I.e. so that the coins must be held in one hand the whole time. "Then hand over the coins to a volunteer.

What you can now observe are signals that always appear in "normal" concentration, but also in situations where someone does something for the first time. (Those who have never performed such tests will notice how little he controls the movements of his finger muscles since he uses the muscles of his hand to hold the coin's thrust!)

5.4.2 The Corners of The Mouth

With the essence of a facial expression probably the corners of the mouth should be. Below are three faces that each have their mouths missing. You should draw this yourself, in particular at A, B, and C the mouth, which is shown under a, b and c:

A. Barely noticeable lifting of the corners of the mouth,

B. Neither a lifting nor a lowering of the same and ultimately

C. Lowered corners of the mouth, also barely noticeable!

If it is extremely amazing how much the overall facial expression is changed, then keep in mind:

In the face mimic expressions of the three areas always apply only in association with each other as signals that can be interpreted.

No one can raise or lower corners of the mouth to a fraction of a millimeter without moving other muscles on the face!

A very happy-satisfied face and a disgustingly disapproving face are very different in terms of the overall signals:

Because of this, the following information we give about the corners of the mouth automatically means that these other signals are always "running."

What the currently compressed mouth means, we have already addressed. Here we are concerned with people whose mouths have been so often compressed that deep lines have formed from the corners of the mouth downwards. Although we have already mentioned that these lines may have been caused by disease or heavy fate, these lines are often the result of a development that could be described as follows: In youth these people still had illusions! (In young people, one can observe that the corners of the mouth tend to move upward.) Then these people lost one illusion after another. They experienced frustrations, they became dissatisfied, they realized more and more, how many of their goals, desires, and hopes slipped away from them. This has embittered them. In the middle years of life, such people often have a thin line where the lips should be. Later, the lowering of the corners of the mouth becomes chronic, but is also accompanied by a squeezing of the lips, an act of strength costs and is generated by the muscle. This process then leads to the deep "notched" lines. So that this chronically compressed mouth can often indicate a disillusioned, dissatisfied, or unhappy person whom it is difficult to "justify" today. Such people are often self-pitying and generally find everything terribly lamentable or "impossible."

But there is another kind of compressed mouth in which the "compressed" mouth is pulled together rather narrow, almost as if one wanted to whistle especially higher notes.

5.4.3 The COMPRESSED MOUTH

In one of his books, Eric BERNE suggests the following experiment, in which not only the facial muscles but also the muscles of the back work with the corners of the mouth in a bandage: sit down (if you are not sitting anyway) and squeeze the anus muscle together. Now lean forward slightly and try to get up without bracing yourself anywhere and without losing control of the tightly contracted anus muscle. Stop.

Well, were you curious enough to give it a try? Then you have determined that the tension has "wandered" over the spine up to your mouth. The slightly contracted and thus slightly tapered mouth is another form of the compressed mouth than the one in which we keep our lips pinch straight and the corners of the mouth. The former form is described in American with the term "tight-ass."

When an American says someone is a "tight ass," he wants to suggest various things: First, this person may be "emotionally cramped," neither open nor spontaneous in his utterances. On the other hand, he may be overly reserved (even stingy), so that the word "restraint" is meant both wisely and figuratively. Ultimately, people are also referred to as those who are close to one another

Adhere to a set of moral rules and at the same time forbid all others to behave more freely. Someone who starts a clean canvas action because he even such "bad" films may not see (because his programs him this prohibit) and now wants to ensure that others should act according to his morality.

Once again, you could see how the vernacular points to connections between physical and emotional tension. When we consider this interdependence of the physical and psyche, does not it fill you with wonder at how wonderful our body works? (Although we know that countless autonomic processes are also affected, such as the resistance of the skin to excitement, hormones are affected by moods and in turn influence those, etc.) That is why I prefer the eastern attitude that does not say "I have «A body, but: I am my body.

Exactly the other person is "his" body. That is why the body always speaks ("with") when we communicate (or are alone). As far as the corners of the mouth are concerned, they are not just a transmitter-instrument (because others of our mouths can "read" an incredible amount - and we of them), but: Here is the context of the mutual influence of physical and psyche most easily understood:

Photo by Stefan Stefancik

The power of smile:...........................

Photo by Guilherme-Stecanella-370455-unsplash

5.4.4 Smile!

In Chinese, it is said: "Who cannot smile should not open a shop."

But that does not mean that the grouchy shopkeeper works negatively on customers (who will not return), but also wants to say something about the mental state of such a person: A person who cannot smile is himself too "not good." He is not in the pure with himself, he does not rest in himself, he is dissatisfied, etc.

But one cannot succeed in becoming self-employed, be it in commerce, industry, the service industry or elsewhere.

That's why American managers not only "fire" salespeople who cannot smile, but also executives! One could almost say: At least from the middle management level hardly people are used whose corners of the mouth chronically "fall"!

Another attempt that will surprise you greatly when you perform it: The next time you really get "sour" out of a conversation and soon have to enter the next conversation situation, try to smile. moving on before the next partner encounter.

In the first approach, of course, the Council sounds absurd. First, you have absolutely no desire to smile, and secondly, you know that you can make a face, but not a smile. Right and wrong.

Right as far as our remarks apply to you. Wrong for another reason: The "grimace," the "tortured smile," the "funny grin," which now comes forcing you to raise the corners of your mouth!

This fact triggers a chain reaction because body language and feelings are always mutually dependent. If you get the "grin" about 20 seconds long to comply, your feeling changes suddenly and quite abruptly! First, your grin seems "weird." It changes into a slightly "torment" over-self-smile, which is almost a "real smile"!

Next, you will find that you can now think more clearly because you are calmer. Again, you often find that the one who annoyed you, either did not know it, did not want it, or at the moment could not do otherwise.

In the meantime, your "smile" has become a shade more "brighter."

If you then turn to the next interlocutor, you will not necessarily spotlight him, but you will not present him with disgusting wrinkles (which, in turn, would have affected his reactions, so that the chance of getting out of this negative feeling would have been far less!)

Chapter 6 - Exercises : "Mirror Test"

Try yourself in front of the mirror... determine what you see and what you can interpret. Compare your interpretation with what your family members see looking at the same thing you see in the mirror

Maintaining a facial expression of interest goes hand in hand with eye contact. Smile naturally because a fake smile shows from afar. You never yawn when someone is talking to you because it is a sure way to demotivate him immediately. Think that much of your success, as we have said, depends on the first meeting and you want others to perceive you as someone alert, attentive, knowledgeable and reliable. Do these two exercises for the next 2 or 3 weeks; They will help you make a good impression:

- Look in the mirror before leaving home and ask yourself:

1. "What message am I sending to people who know me for the first time?"

2. "What opinions will they have of me before I open my mouth?"

- Get more knowledge of your body language by asking your friends, family, mentors and colleagues to tell you what you are saying without speaking.

Instead of the mirror, you can also use a video camera to capture your image and then analyze it and interpret it alone or with others. This is really a nice experiment to do in company, in an evening with friends where each of you can analyze others. There is a lot of fun.

Now that you know this exercise (a very interesting and fun one to do it on your own or socially... you'll see how nice is it!!!), it is useful to re-read the parts of the book and the examples that need a visual approach and to repeat the "Mirror Test" after this reading. Performing the test you will learn very quickly how to really control your body language, becoming a communication professional, you will become able to observe the improvements by training and performing the test after some time, don't underestimate this great practical exercise!!!

Chapter 7 - 10 Tips To Make A Good First Impression

In the first encounter the brain quickly assimilates a huge amount of information about the person. This first impression never changed again in 80%-90% of the time as it is very complicated for the brain to change the cognitive construction that has been achieved during the first encounter....during the first half hour of conversation. We are going to offer you 10 tips/tricks, some of which can be considered as a summary of what has already been discussed in the book. Reiterating some examples and considerations once again is actually very useful for the reading and learning process in the reader's memory. In this way some key concepts of communication are fixed and easily and subconsciously usable. In this way, if kept in mind in the head, they can over time lead to the spontaneous and automatic implementation of winning communication mechanisms.

Whether you like it or not, there are situations in life where it is important to make a good first impression. If what you want is to get that job that you want so much, or not to throw away the first date with the boy or girl for whom you have spent so many hours sighing, you better keep reading this chapter.

And, in this type of situation, you probably only have a single opportunity to project a good impression. People form opinions of others with just a few minutes, and that is why you should be prepared to show your best version. This does not mean that you should appear to be a top executive when you are not. But even so, being yourself, the attitude or nerves can play tricks on you.

Science has shown that the first impression is achieved in just seven seconds since you meet someone. Therefore, when you meet new people, they make you a quick scanner of your smile, your way of shaking hands, how to introduce yourself, and so on. As the minutes go by, they are thinking about whether you are trustworthy, if you are genuinely a good person, if they want to continue meeting you or if they want to continue working with you. As you can see, many questions are answered in those critical minutes. What they see of you and what you make them feel, will mark if they continue to have contact with you or not.

7.1 Tips To Make A Good First Impression

People can forget what you said. People can forget what you have done. But they will never forget how you made them feel. Think about it for a few seconds, you also form a first impression of the people you meet for the first time, so you should know that. on occasion, and you will have been wrong judging others ahead of time.

To prevent this from happening to you, we invite you to follow the following tips.

7.1.1 Be Punctual

First of all, you must be punctual. Nobody likes to be late for the person they have met, let alone if it is a job interview. Be aware of this and give yourself enough time to arrive on time because, otherwise, you may not have a second chance.

7.1.2 Watch Body Language

Your body language speaks silently about you. Several studies have shown that it is four times more important than the things you can say. Looking at the person's eyes while talking or shaking hands firmly is important to make a good first impression.

7.1.3 Smile

Although the smile has to do with body language, separating it from the previous point is important to remember. You don't need to show your teeth, but there's nothing that creates a better impression than a big smile. Try not to go from the smile to seriousness very quickly, it will seem that you are forcing it. The key is in naturalness.

7.1.4 Relax

The posture is important to show good body language, but don't look like a robot when trying to control it. Sit straight, but don't be so rigid that you notice that you force the situation. Relax and don't be nervous, enjoy the moment.

7.1.5 Be Yourself

Do not pretend to be someone you are not, because you may notice. So be yourself. This may sound like a topic but it is the truth. So try not to lie, because if you get caught, the image of a liar will be marked.

7.1.6 Be Positive

Your attitude shows in everything you do. Project a positive attitude, even if you receive criticism or are nervous. If you have an interview or have been with that special someone, you should think that if for some reason the situation does not go as you wanted, it will be a great learning.

7.1.7 Trust Yourself

This point brings together all the previous ones, because if you trust yourself, your body language projects it: you smile more, shake hands firmly, you are relaxed, etc. Consequently, it is not only a matter of being forcedly relaxed, but you should value yourself. If not, you may succeed in the first meeting, but little by little your lack of confidence will gain ground.

7.1.8 Be Open And Humble

Humility is one of the values that human beings most appreciate. Try not to be arrogant and be open to others. That creates trust, and a good rapport. A great ego can create rejection, so if you want to fall fast, show yourself as a humble and respectful person.

7.1.9 Highlight Your Features

We have something unique to offer. Perhaps you are an expert in a branch of knowledge that generates curiosity in others, or has a great sense of humor. If you still don't know what you can offer, you better do a self-knowledge job right now. Now, seducing a girl or a boy is not the same as seducing an interviewer for a job. So you must also take into account the situation of each moment.

7.1.10 Be Empathetic

To get along with others, you must be empathetic. This means that if you look at the situation from the point of view of others, you will be closer to knowing exactly how to act and leave a good impression on that person.

7.2   5   Essential   Steps   To   Master Nonverbal Communication

The mastery of nonverbal behavior is essential to effectively manage communication. Learning to manage nonverbal communication skillfully is much easier than it seems, although it requires time and dedication. It requires having awareness and patience, open- mindedness, humility, and a self-critical spirit that is vanity proof. Perhaps that is why most of our leaders dispense with this training, which in my opinion should be given from the first cycles of school education.

Studies says that we don't follow great leaders so much for what they say, as for what they are, for what they do. Words are important, of course, but the facts are more important, because that is the system our brain uses to learn: observe behaviors and imitate them.

As children, our natural tendency is not to do what they tell us (don't get on there, don't scream, don't run, ...), but do what we see. We learn to be people by modeling other people, and when an image or behavior is attractive to us, we tend to identify with its owner.

I will not deceive you. Shortcuts do not exist when it comes to becoming a good communicator. And less, when it comes to building a leadership from nothing. There are also no magic formulas or instant remedies, but those who wish to succeed in the corporate world should keep the machetes and take these five essential steps into account:

7.2.1 First, Know Yourself

Self-diagnosis is the first step in the path of winning communication, says consultant Fran Carrillo. If a person does not know who he is, he can hardly tell and transmit it to others, I add. Being aware of your own behavior, and the effect it produces on your environment, is the beginning of a solid formation.

7.2.2 Do Not Change Your Personality, Perfect Your Style

If you dedicate yourself to your work, you have to observe yourself with a critical spirit and correct everything that squeaks. The mirror serves to rehearse, but it will deceive you. If you want to understand how others see you, try to be videotaped without knowing it and analyze yourself without complacency. You will see what a surprise you get. Change everything that takes you away from your goal. It is not a matter of transforming personality, but of improving style.

7.2.3 Don't Think About The Lyrics, Feel The Music

Understanding the lyrics of the song is important to convey emotions, but what will really make you dance will always be the music. If you have to think about the steps every time you go out on the track, you will most likely stumble or end up stepping on your partner. You have to train and rehearse the corrections one and a thousand times until they go out alone, spontaneously and naturally.

7.2.4 Your Body Is The Message Only If The Message Exists

A person without ideas is like a dancer without choreography or an actor without a script. No matter how well you express yourself, no matter how much your appearance helps you, no matter how attractive you are, without a message to convey and an emotion to share, you are nobody. And if that emotional message does not match your way of being and acting, you will be less than anyone else. Always remember: congruence between who you are, what you do and what you look like.

7.2.5 The Important Thing Is Not The Mistakes, But How You React To Them

And finally, do not go through life in a hammer plan, because everything will seem like nails. A defensive attitude will make you see the questions as threats and the replies as aggressions, your limbic system will kidnap you and you will return blows that you have not even received. Even the most adverse scenario may be the best opportunity to show the behavior that has taken so much effort to train. It is a matter of perspective, accept mistakes normally, rectify and learn.

Chapter 8 - Body Language In Different Parts Of The World

The same gestures can mean different things in different countries. You can even do something considered inappropriate without even realizing it. Although most of the local people do not give importance to certain behaviors because they know you are not from there and you do not have to know ... Wouldn't you rather know them all just in case? We leave you here a fairly detailed list of "etiquette" tips to survive the world without being considered rude or borderline.

1. In some parts of Asia, it is super bad if you touch another person with your foot, since it is the lowest part of the body. Do not point to objects or people with your feet, or put your feet on chairs or tables. Feet, use them to walk. It is also rude to point out just as we do, with the index finger. Especially in

Singapore, instead of pointing that finger, do it with your thumb. It seems stupid, but it is more polite.

2. Also in Asia, it is frowned upon to touch people on the head or to dishevel them. The head is spiritually the highest part of the body. You do not sit on cushions or pillows that are intended to support the head, it is another type of offense.

3. In certain parts of Asia, such as in Singapore, it is very bad to leave the sticks with which you eat pointing at someone. It means you wish him evil!

4. It is also dangerous using the thumb up sign. Just as in most of the world it is well seen to indicate that something is right, in places like Thailand, Iran or Iraq it is an obscene sign and you should never do it. Basically it means, put it somewhere.

5. In Nepal, it is impolite to pass over someone's legs (In narrow places where there are people sitting, for example). Avoid doing so and remove your legs when

someone wants to pass. Nor do you sit or stand on a cushion belonging to a monk, even if there is no one sitting on it. In the Tibetan Temples (Stupas/chortens) always walk clockwise or they will look strange.

6. In Japanese baths, called Onsen, you should wash yourself before getting into the water. It seems silly but they consider the water to be contaminated if you don't do it that way. In addition, you should put a cloth or something that covers your noble parts.

7. People in Spain and Italy are quite expressive. They have cheek kisses, hugs and constant physical contact when they talk to another person. It's very good, but don't think that the rest of the world is like that!

8. In Russia, shaking hands on the threshold of a door is considered bad luck. As a curious fact we will say that if a pizza maker comes to your door, you will have to go out to get the pizza or you will have to

invite him in, but he will refuse to give it to you right at the door's threshold!

9. In India you can make a compliment without even opening your mouth. If someone approaches you by placing your tongue between your teeth (It sounds a bit weird but it is like that) and gesturing with your arms as if including you in your personal space, it is that it finds you incredibly beautiful or very intelligent.

10. In England, showing the index and middle fingers with the palm facing inwards is the equivalent of a Spanish sleeve cut (only with the middle finger). It is strongly recommended not to order two coffees with that gesture. Doing it with the palm out (Victoria or Peace), is the right way to do it

11. In Morocco a greeting can last up to 10 minutes! After shaking hands, the Moroccans touch their hearts as if to imply that they do it "really", that they are really glad to see you. Also for courtesy they

throw themselves a while asking questions of the type How are you? All good? I hope your parents are well.

12. In Bulgaria, it is important to know that to say yes, the head moves from side to side, and to say no, from top to bottom. These Bulgarians are crazy!

13. In many countries in Africa, it is rude to look directly into the eyes of your elders. It is a sign of respect not to do so, just like sitting at the table before them. They must be the first to sit and the first to speak.

14. Never touch a Muslim woman when she is introduced to you, do not even offer her hand to give it to her. And if you are a woman, never touch a Buddhist monk.

15. In some countries in Asia, it is polite to take and offer things with both hands.

Conclusion

Thank you for reading to the end of *Body Language*. We hope it was informative and provided you with the tools you will need to achieve your goals, whatever they may be.

We hope you enjoyed reading this book. This book will serve as a guide to interpreting others' actions and understanding what you convey through your own body language.

You will be able to better understand body language and what people around you are communicating through their nonverbal gestures and expressions.

There is no doubt that humans are social beings. In other words, we depend on each other and interact constantly. To be able to interact, we need to communicate. We are all aware of our ability to communicate verbally, but few of us notice the unspoken language we use when talking to others.

Do not wait any longer! Begin the journey that will take you to the life you have always dreamed of.

Finally, if you found this book useful in any way, a review on Amazon is always appreciated!

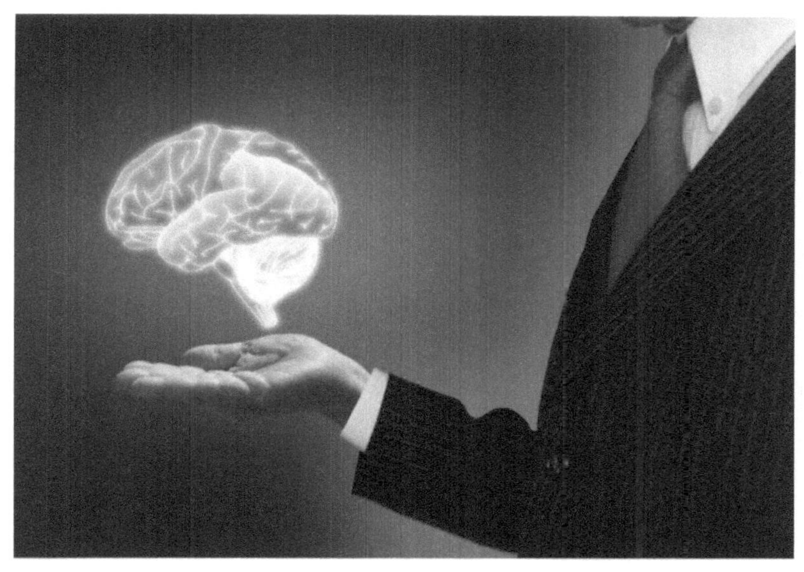

I say what I think with the mouth and my body!!!

The failure of a relationship is almost always a communication failure.

(Zygmunt Bauman)

.... but YOU will never fail your communication again!!!

Edward J.P. Aniston

Search others publications by author: "Edward J.P. Aniston"
on Amazon.com and Audible.com , thanks!